STAND
STRONG
AMERICA

STAND STRONG AMERICA

Courage, Freedom, and Hope for Tomorrow

Jason Jimenez • Alex McFarland

BroadStreet
PUBLISHING

BroadStreet Publishing Group, LLC
Racine, Wisconsin, USA
BroadStreetPublishing.com

Stand Strong America: Courage, Freedom, and Hope for Tomorrow

Copyright © 2016 Jason Jimenez and Alex McFarland

ISBN-13: 978-1-4245-5242-9 (softcover)
ISBN-13: 978-1-4245-5243-6 (e-book)

Stock or custom editions of BroadStreet Publishing titles may be purchased in bulk for educational, business, ministry, fundraising, or sales promotional use. For information, please e-mail info@broadstreetpublishing.com.

Cover design by Chris Garborg at garborgdesign.com
Interior design and typeset by Katherine Lloyd at theDESKonline.com

Printed in the United States of America
16 17 18 19 20 5 4 3 2 1

CONTENTS

INTRODUCTION

America hangs in the balance. Established on the ideals and principles of Christianity, the world now looks on as America, the once glorious beacon on the hill, sheds its dependency on God. The once unwavering allegiance to the self-evident truths of God is now considered a nuisance to America's progress. In fact, if America breaks away from its Christian heritage, the future of our great nation will undoubtedly end. Proverbs 29:2 reminds us, "When the righteous thrive, the people rejoice; when the wicked rule, the people groan."

America has been ruled by wickedness for far too long, and the results are catastrophic. Over a million unborn babies are aborted each year (it is estimated that 2,800–4,000 babies are aborted each day, and this is being paid for by us—the taxpayers). Marriage has now been redefined by a 5–4 Supreme Court vote. Our national debt has grown to almost $20 trillion. Civil unrest is breaking out in communities all across the country. Drug use, porn addiction, and human trafficking are on the rise. On top of all of this, many Americans are fleeing to Syria, Iran, and Iraq to be trained by ISIS. And free speech and religious freedom are being undermined more and more by an out-of-control government.

Yet there is still hope. There is still a window of opportunity to reignite our country's fervor to bring peace and regain stability once again in America. But it will require something—something more than what the majority of Americans are willing to give. Americans must be willing to take a stand on behalf of our freedoms. Just as it took a great struggle to bring freedom to the colonists, so it will take commitment and valor to *preserve* our liberties as well.

At his inauguration as the first president of the United States, George Washington said, "The sacred fire of liberty has been entrusted to the American people."[1] To be entrusted with something means that we are then responsible for taking care of what has been entrusted to us. Similarly, we have been entrusted with the task to speak and spread God's truth. We have a sacred obligation to stand for what is right despite the backlash or the cost. If we want to see America rise up from the ashes of death, then we (even if it starts with a small few) must be willing to lay down our lives and pray to God for the courage to fight for future generations.

The great American poet Robert Frost said, "Freedom lies in being bold."[2] We must boldly seek God for the strength needed to fight for the freedoms bestowed on us by God, and not for one second to abandon the call to challenge and engage our culture with the gospel of Jesus Christ. It is vital that young people know that we care, and that they witness firsthand what it looks like to live free and moral lives unto God.

The time to stand up for biblical truth is now. In fact, we would argue that the posterity of the Christian faith depends on it. We must stop ignoring our responsibility, and start solving the problems that are destroying our nation. If you care about America and the future impact Christianity will have on generations to come, then it's time to stand strong for America.

Our second president, John Adams, once said, "Posterity! You will never know how much it cost the present generation to secure your freedom. … I hope you will make good use of it."[3] More than two-hundred years later, these words come to *our* generation as a challenge to make good use of what has been paved in blood for us. Together we can build a better tomorrow by living out our faith today.

CHAPTER 1

HOW CHRISTIANITY SHAPED AMERICA'S FOUNDATION

Blessed is the nation whose God is the LORD.

—PSALM 33:12

You've seen the news headlines: A city courthouse will no longer display the Ten Commandments; a school will no longer include Christmas carols with religious lyrics; a state capital will no longer allow a nativity scene on its property. Today's increasingly post-Christian, secular environment seeks to remove any and all religious influence from every area of public life. Yet America would not exist without Christianity and the godly lives of its early citizens.

For example, in his inaugural speech George Washington stated, "If I could have entertained the slightest apprehension that the Constitution which was framed in our convention, where I had the honor of presiding, might possibly endanger the religious rights of any ecclesiastical society [that is, a church or denomination], certainly, I would never have placed my signature upon it."[1] Our nation's first president understood, and publically proclaimed, the importance of religious freedom. This was not to exclude faith from public life; rather, it was to offer the maximum amount of freedom for those who sought to worship God.

And George Washington was not alone in his quest to encourage American citizens to freely worship the God of the Bible. James Madison, the fourth president of our nation, served as chief architect of the US Constitution. He once noted:

> We have staked the whole future of American civilization, not upon the power of government, far from it. We have staked the future of all our political institutions upon the capability of mankind for self-government; upon the capacity of each and all of us to govern ourselves, to control ourselves, to sustain ourselves according to the Ten Commandments of God.[2]

Madison's goal was freedom, including freedom to worship according to the commands of God's Word.

In 1831, French writer Alexis de Tocqueville traveled to America to observe the power of its increasing greatness among nations. He noted in his two-volume work, *Democracy in America*, "There is no country in the world where the Christian religion retains a greater influence over the souls of men, than in America."[3] His investigation noted that the key to America's greatness and freedom could be found in its faith.

Why Does This Matter?

We (Alex and Jason) often discover people who fail to see the importance of studying America's Christian heritage. Many people tend to focus on the here and now—the latest smartphone or the most recent news headline. So why does it matter whether or not we know about America's spiritual foundations?

I (Alex) will admit, I once fell into the category of those who cared more about what was happening now and little about the past of our nation. However, all of this changed in college when I first seriously encountered American history. What began as a course to complete a requirement introduced me to a world of powerful leaders and a godly legacy I had failed to previously recognize.

Furthermore, I realized that many of the events recorded throughout our nation's history have repeated themselves in various forms. For example, Lincoln's assassination during the era of the Civil War strangely resembled the assassination attempt on President Ronald Reagan during the Cold War. When President George W. Bush and New York Mayor Rudy Giuliani rallied Americans in unity following the attacks of 9/11, their words often reflected the attitudes of Americans following the attack on Pearl Harbor in 1941 that led to the nation's entry into World War II.

Thirdly, I realized the tremendous influence of Christianity in the founding of America. I had heard about the Puritans and knew the Pledge of Allegiance included "one nation under God," but the stories behind this history forced me to grow in my own faith. Would I have responded as these brave men and women did so long ago?

We often fail to recognize the many ways in which Christianity has influenced America. A quick look reveals twelve key areas in which our faith has had tremendous influence on our society today.

1. *Human Rights.* People are created in the image of God and are equal in His sight, which is something affirmed in our nation's Constitution.
2. *Women's Rights.* Still today, it is illegal for women to drive in Saudi Arabia. Why is this? It is simply because the nation does not have a Christian worldview regarding women's rights. Instead, America offers equality for women, and, though far from perfect, it far exceeds the rights of women in non-Christian societies.
3. *The Rights of Children.* Christianity has caused many to join the pro-life movement to save the lives of the

preborn. Historically, Christian convictions have also been behind the creation of child labor laws, Christian schools, increased emphasis on education, and social services to help children in need, whether due to abuse, special needs, disability, or any other need.

4. *The End of Slavery and Legalized Discrimination.* On the negative side, it is true some have used the Bible to justify slavery and racism. However, it is also true that it has been Christians who have led the way to end slavery and legalized discrimination. For example, Martin Luther King Jr. was known as a Baptist minister long before he was known as a civil rights activist.

5. *Education.* America's earliest schools were held in churches. In fact, Christians started the first colleges in America, including Harvard, to further higher education and to train ministers.

6. *Health Care.* Still today, some of the most notable hospitals in our nation include the names Baptist, Methodist, or Presbyterian at the end, acknowledging the fact that they were started by churches and Christian organizations.

7. *Marriage and Family.* Christian convictions regarding marriage focused on heterosexual monogamous love and the rearing of children within a marriage relationship.

8. *Government.* Fifty of the fifty-five signers of the US Constitution were Christians. The concept of checks and balances and many other aspects of our founders' beliefs were based on biblical concepts. Still today, the Liberty Bell reminds us of the Bible's influence through its inscription of Leviticus 25:10, which reads in our modern translation: "Proclaim liberty throughout the land unto all the inhabitants thereof."

9. *Science*. The scientific revolution that has so influenced our nation's economic and educational advancements developed prior to Darwinian theory, building its basis upon a God who created all things—even rational truth and scientific laws.

10. *Free Enterprise*. Where Christianity exists as the predominant religion, free enterprise is generally the result. The Protestant work ethic that was popularized by John Calvin during the Reformation became the basis for America's system of work and employment.

11. *The Arts*. Many of America's greatest artists, musicians, and literary geniuses have been people of the Christian faith. Even much of America's early architecture was inspired by Christian religious themes.

12. *Foreign Relations*. America has long served as a leader among the world's nations. This is greatly influenced by the Christian beliefs of loving one's neighbor as one's self as well as belief in the Great Commission to make disciples of all nations. Furthermore, American Christianity, despite its flaws, has led the modern missionary revolution. In addition, Christians working in foreign relations in American government have had great influence to often improve the lives of those in other nations, encouraging democracy and peace, and offering humanitarian aid to those in need.

Our hope is that these twelve themes that have shaped our own faith will influence your faith as well. When we encounter the importance that faith has made in the lives of the early influencers of our nation, we can then learn how to better influence our nation—and our world.

Fascinating Facts about Christopher Columbus

One important example is found in the life of Christopher Columbus. Modern historians realize Europeans and other travelers visited America prior to Christopher Columbus in 1492. However, many do not realize the spiritual background of his writings upon his voyage to this new world. He wrote in *Columbus's Book of Prophecies*:

> It was the Lord who put into my mind that it would be possible to sail from here to the Indies. All who heard of my project rejected it with laughter, ridiculing me.
>
> There is no question that the inspiration was from the Holy Spirit, because He comforted me with rays of marvelous illumination from the Holy Scriptures. ... Our Redeemer Jesus Christ said that before the end of the world, all things must come to pass that had been written by the prophets. Isaiah goes into great detail in describing future events and in calling all people to our holy catholic [universal] faith. Most of the prophecies of Holy Scripture have been fulfilled already. ...
>
> For the execution of the journey to the Indies, I did not make use of intelligence, mathematics, or maps. It is simply the fulfillment of what Isaiah prophesied. All this is what I desire to write down for you in this book.
>
> These are great and wonderful things for the earth, and the signs are that the Lord is hastening the end. The fact that the Gospel must still be preached to so many lands in such a short time, this is what convinces me.[4]

Columbus saw his travels as a calling from the Lord. He had studied the Bible and believed his work was part of the fulfillment of God's plan to bring the gospel message to the ends of the earth. While modern historians often only note Columbus as an explorer, he certainly also viewed himself as a missionary.

Elsewhere Columbus viewed himself as a "Servant of the Most High Savior, Christ, the Son of Mary." Columbus's personal log stated his purpose in seeking undiscovered worlds: "[To] bring the Gospel of Jesus Christ to the heathens. ... [To] bring the Word of God to unknown coastlands.... To bear the light of Christ west to the heathen undiscovered lands."[5]

Columbus filled pages of his logbooks with scriptural passages and allusions. He loved to apply Bible verses to what he was experiencing in his own life. He was especially moved by the book of Isaiah, and viewed his voyages as the fulfillment of prophecy that would lead to the return of Jesus.

Christopher Columbus also frequently quoted Matthew 28:19–20 and Acts 1:8 in relation to himself. He believed that God had a divine plan for the North American continent, and that he was a part of that plan. While many seek to remove Columbus Day from the calendar, we find reason to celebrate the life of a man who sought to honor God through his character and work.

The Example of George Washington

We remember George Washington as America's first president, but those who lived during his lifetime likely remembered him for his faith. Did you know that Washington's first official act after being sworn in as president was to join all the members of the House and Senate in a two-hour worship service? A similar action today would shock our modern media. Could you imagine the next president of the United States calling Congress for a church service? Yet Washington was known for such acts of devotion.

Another example can be found in Washington's first Thanksgiving proclamation that was given on October 3, 1789. In it he stated, "It is the duty of all nations to acknowledge the providence of Almighty God, to obey His will, to be grateful for His benefits and humbly to implore His protection and favor."[6]

The Examples of the Early States

The late James D. Kennedy offers several examples from the history of the early American states to show the influence of Christianity upon those states. For example, Delaware stated, "The duty of all men frequently to assemble together for the public worship of the Author of the Universe"; and its oath of office included, "I do profess faith in God the Father, and in Jesus Christ His only Son, and in the Holy Ghost, one God blessed forever more." Maryland noted that "the legislature may ... lay a general and equal tax for the support of the Christian religion," and the state even required a "declaration of belief in the Christian religion" from all of its state officers. Massachusetts directed local political bodies to "make suitable provisions, at their own expense, for the institution of public worship of God," while North Carolina declared "no person who shall deny the being of God, or the divine authority of the Old and New Testament ... shall be capable of holding office or place of trust ... within this state."[7]

North Carolina is an important state for me (Alex) because it is where I was born and where I continue to call home today. Yet it was not until recently that I learned the true history of my state's founding. Originally part of Virginia, North Carolina had been granted to Sir Robert Heath in 1629. Virginia was named after the "Virgin Queen," Elizabeth I, by Sir Walter Raleigh, who explored the area and attempted to found a settlement on Roanoke Island in 1585.

On August 13, 1587, the members of the colony converted the Native American named Manteo, who was then baptized into the Christian faith. That same month the first child was born in America, and she was baptized Virginia Dare. But it was not until the 1650s that English colonists began to settle North Carolina permanently.

In the Charter of Carolina in 1663, which was granted by King Charles II, Sir William Berkeley, and the seven other Lord Proprietors, it is written:

Being excited with a laudable and pious zeal for the propaga-
tion [spreading] of the Christian faith … they have humbly
besought leave of us, to transport and make an ample colony,
in the parts of America not yet cultivated or planted, and only
inhabited by some barbarous people, who have no knowledge
of Almighty God.[8]

Notice that the fundamental reason for exploration and settling
the area known as Carolina was not financial but for the spread of
the Christian faith.

Here's where many modern historians find a point of controversy, however. The colonists were met by Native Americans who
worshiped various spirits. Did the colonists recognize the existing
paganism as alternative spiritualities that were equally valid with
Christianity? Of course they didn't. And was the public expression
of Christian theism discouraged in order to not offend other religious groups? Absolutely not.

The state charter implicitly recognizes only the God of Christian
theism. In the public and private writings from our formative days,
the terms *Almighty God* and *Divine Being* were specifically used in
reference to the God of the Bible. While the founders vehemently
opposed the establishment of one national church or denomination, the acceptance of Christianity was universally acknowledged.

In fact, the Fundamental Constitution of the Carolinas (1663)
directly stated: "No man shall be permitted to be a freeman [res-
ident, landowner] of Carolina or to have any estate of habitation
within it that doth not acknowledge a God, and that God is pub-
licly and solemnly to be worshipped."[9]

The first governor, William Sayle, was a Nonconformist who
allowed religious toleration for all denominations. Of the many
Christians who began to settle in North Carolina beginning in
1653, the Quaker missionaries were among the most notable, with
even George Fox, the founder of Quakerism, preaching there. At

a later date, the Quaker family of Daniel Boone, along with other Quaker families, pioneered the Yadkin River Valley along the North Carolina frontier. The first Baptist congregation was formed there in 1727, and was followed later by Methodist congregations, who recognized African Americans as ministers and strongly preached against slavery.

The Constitution of the State of North Carolina (1776) would later note, "There shall be no establishment of any one religious church or denomination in this State, in preference to any other." And Article XXXII declares:

> That no person who shall deny the Being of God or the truth of the Protestant religion, or the Divine Authority of the Old or New Testaments, or who shall hold religious principles incompatible with the freedom and safety of State, shall be capable of holding any office or place of trust or profit in the civil department within this State.[10]

The Preamble of the North Carolina State Constitution (1868) expresses its Christian heritage with these words:

> We the people of the State of North Carolina, grateful to Almighty God, the Sovereign Ruler of Nations, for the preservation of the American Union and the existence of our civil, political, and religious liberties, and acknowledging our dependence upon Him for the continuance of those blessings to us and our posterity, do, for the more certain security thereof and for the better government of this State, ordain and establish this Constitution.

Other American colonies and states include similar words in their founding documents, thus demonstrating the unmistakable presence of a Christian worldview in the minds and intents of America's founders.

An Example for Today

Why do these examples matter for us today? Let us share a few reasons. First, we can change the future by learning from the past. Why did the early American colonies, states, and leaders rise to such greatness? One fundamental reason is the widely shared Christian faith among America's early people. While not perfect, these men and women led based on biblical convictions we can learn from today.

Second, we need to know the whole story. From textbooks to sound bites, today's thought leaders seek to rewrite or suppress aspects of faith from America's history. We are not a nation of imperialist capitalists who came to a new world to colonize and make a buck. America's founders largely moved to this land for religious freedom.

Third, America needs a renewed story. We all know about terrorism, crime, and moral decay, but what our country requires is a solution beyond politics and policies. No law or leader will return America to greatness, but God's law and godly leaders can lead us back in that direction. If we choose to live out God's truths in our own lives, we can join in the legacy of America's godly leaders who shape a nation through character and conviction.

As I (Alex) noted in a recent commentary, while the rhetoric of "life, liberty and the pursuit of happiness" is still politically correct, any recognition that life and liberty are gifts from God and God alone have become unbearable to those who would seek to eradicate God from American history and life.[11] Political correctness is the banner of cowards. It's time for our nation, and each of us as its citizens, to reject the fear of giving offense. We must stand up and call for national repentance and prayer, and not the politically correct homogenized prayers designed to placate special-interest groups, but prayers to the God of the Bible, whose protection and blessing are the only reason our nation still exists.

Life and liberty are at risk today. It's because, as a nation, we have forgotten and even rejected our source, author, and giver—almighty God. Some think we can continue to enjoy our freedoms apart from God, but if we don't realize the fallacy of this belief, we will soon lose our freedoms and the protections of the God who gave them.

Time is running out. We have been blessed by God, but it's critical that we understand that God does not owe us anything at all. If we continue as a nation to reject God, then we fool ourselves into thinking He is obligated to bless, prosper, or protect us. Let us turn to God once again, recognizing He is the giver of every blessing and freedom we currently enjoy.

CHAPTER 2

DREAMS
OF OUR FATHERS

Having undertaken for the Glory of God,
and Advancement of the Christian Faith …
—THE MAYFLOWER COMPACT

On this historical ship—the *Mayflower*—was a group of Puritans who personified great courage, faith, and determination. Their resolve was to be set free from the abuses and corruption of the Church of England, a course that would one day revolutionize the New World.

The Puritans (who were also known as Saints or Separatists) stood out among the rest for their disapproval of the Church of England. They rejected the tyrannical rule of James I and showed much disdain for the Catholic persuasion on the Anglican Church. However, their attempts to reform the church from within had little influence. They were considered outcasts and perceived as a growing threat. However, despite the increased persecution, the Puritans' devotion to the Christian faith remained strong—so strong, in fact, that they were willing to abandon their homeland and even risk death.

It was in the year 1608 that their bold faith and undying resilience to be free sprang to action. Under the direction of John Robinson, 125 Puritans secretly fled from the brutal dictatorship of England to Holland. They knew Holland was not their final destination but indeed a step closer to fulfilling their hopeful dream—to one day be free from tyranny and establish their own "holy commonwealths" in America.

For many, the past twelve years in Holland was tolerable, yet it came with hardships. Jobs were scarce, making it difficult for the Puritans to provide for their families. Those who did find work labored tirelessly to bring home what little they could earn. The Dutch culture also grew to be a bad influence on the Puritan children and was a matter of grave concern. Nonetheless, Holland was a great test for the Puritans. It not only strengthened their faith but also kept them from giving up. Notwithstanding the strict laws and the previous failed attempts that landed some in jail, the Puritans pressed on and believed God for a miracle. They strongly believed that if their children were to have futures filled with freedom, then God would make a way for them to set sail to the New World.

Remarkably, after much prayer and persuading certain authorities, the Puritans received permission from the London Company to voyage across the Atlantic Ocean to Virginia. This certainly was an answer to prayer, but it offered no firm guarantees. The Puritans would still have to consider how they would survive the rough passage to such a faraway land.

Knowing the risks, they bravely moved forward to go to America. For them, risking their lives so that their children and their future generations would be free from tyranny and war was worth the cost of life. America was now their hope; it was their God-given destiny.

Sailing to the New World

And so the Puritans, now called the "Pilgrims," sailed to the New World in search of a newfound life that would permit them the freedom to live out their Christian beliefs as they desired. But to meet the uncertainties that lie ahead, the Puritans would need a leader of unprecedented measure. Reluctantly, their search did not take them long.

Born in the remote village of Austerfield, Yorkshire, in England, William Bradford (1590–1657), one of the original 125 Separatists who fled to Holland back in 1608, would take on the role as the Puritans' leader—he would become one of America's most legendary pioneers. Now all that remained was to get on the *Mayflower* and arrive safely in America.

On September 16, 1620, Bradford and thirty-four other original Puritans (from 1608) set sail from England. However, the journey would not be an easy one. The elements of the sea were merciless on the ship as well as the people and the crew on board—many underwent severe seasickness.

Long into the journey, the *Mayflower* suffered a massive blow from a gigantic wave, causing structural damage to the topside of the ship. Christopher Jones, the *Mayflower*'s master, felt obliged to turn back the ship for fear they wouldn't reach America. However, with weeks already into the journey, the Pilgrims believed that God would overcome any adversity they faced. They trusted God wouldn't have gotten them this far just to have them turn back. Sure, they knew the risk was great, but the reward was far greater.

Finally, after sixty-five long and harsh days, the 102 people aboard the *Mayflower* landed at Plymouth in Cape Cod, on November 21, 1620. But the excitement of arriving to America was short lived. Rather than arriving in Virginia in the heat of summer, they landed hundreds of miles off course at the beginning of winter. At this point of the journey, two people had died and many more aboard the ship were plagued with fatal illnesses. Very little food and water remained. In the first year, over half of the 102 people who arrived on the *Mayflower* had died, and yet, despite the hunger, despair, and harsh conditions, the remaining few Puritans found a way to survive.

Notwithstanding the many deaths that occurred on the *May-flower*, this voyage set the mark for many more to come. It was on this voyage that the Mayflower Compact was drafted and signed on November 11, 1620. This historic document was the first of its kind to establish the equal rights contract under the division and power of the God of Christianity, and would later be incorporated into the US Constitution.

A City upon a Hill

Several years later, King Charles I (who succeeded James I) authorized a joint-stock company (Massachusetts Bay Company) in 1629 to establish a colony in New England. John Winthrop was selected to lead the voyage of over a thousand Puritans (including men, women, and children) on seventeen ships headed for the New World. This voyage was what Winthrop had prayed for.

The unruly behavior of the king and corruption of the Church drove Winthrop to take his family and others to explore the opportunity to live a life of religious freedom, just as William Bradford and the Puritans did before him. Determined for a new start, Governor Winthrop and his colony of Puritans left England on May 22, 1630, and carried westward across the Atlantic.

On board the *Arabella*, Winthrop wrote the famed document entitled *A Model of Christian Charity*. In it, he wrote about their cause before God: "Thus stands the cause between God and us. We are entered into covenant with Him for this work. We have taken out a commission." He went on to write these profound words:

> For we must consider that we shall be as a city upon a hill.
> The eyes of all people are upon us. So that if we shall deal
> falsely with our God in this work we have undertaken, and so
> cause Him to withdraw His present help from us, we shall be
> made a story and a by-word through the world.[1]

Winthrop closed his message by affirming, "Therefore let us choose life, that we and our seed may live, by obeying His voice and cleaving to Him, for He is our life and our prosperity."[2]

On June 12, 1630, Winthrop and his people arrived and established the Massachusetts Bay Colony. Governor Winthrop's *A Model of Christian Charity* had a lasting impact on the Puritans, for it set the mark for their arrival and helped the people accomplish God's will for them in the New World.

Corporate Life of Family

Henry Drummond stated, "The family circle is the supreme conductor of Christianity."[3] One thing clearly illustrated in Puritan life was the involvement of the family. Wherever the Puritans went and whatever the Puritans did, their family was at the center of it all. It didn't matter if they were working out in the fields, sewing clothes, attending school, selling produce in the market, or representing their constituents in political life—the corporate life of family remained strong.

Take a look at families in America today. Families are broken—broken down and biblically illiterate. Divorce is the norm, and family values have all but been lost. There needs to be a move of God to rebuild marriages and families today—and not just any kind of family. We are talking about the biblical model of marriage and family. We are not talking about same-sex families, and not cohabiting families, but the union between one man and one woman for a lifetime. What we need is strong families with a father and a mother, allowing us to get back to the model God created.

Families that rely powerfully on God and seek to do His will be blessed in all that they do. A united marriage that stays together will be united with the purpose to produce a strong family. These attributes were at the core of the Puritan life and family. And if we don't return to this way of life, then the continual breakdown of the family will eventually lead to the destruction of our nation. It's not money, jobs, or government that prosper a nation; rather, it's families transformed by the gospel of Jesus Christ and devoted to the cause that prosper a nation.

Can you imagine what will become of our society, and even our nation, if future generations cease to produce biblical families? Instead of dwelling on the woes of tomorrow, what can you do to help restore families? The truth is that if you want to see families restored, then it *must* start with you. Don't wait for your pastor or church to do something about the family—don't sit around and complain about the problems that are prevalent in our society. Do something about it.

Be that person—be that godly couple—willing to step up and step out to help those who are in need. There are so many single homes who need godly couples to come alongside them and help them; to comfort them and to give them advice; to take on some of the challenges they face alone.

You see, we have overlooked the greatest mission field in our culture today: the family. We need to be reminded that family is the first and most meaningful institution created by God. But don't start and stop with yourself, as if you take care of your family and that is enough. Rather, start praying for more mentor couples to take more families under their wings; start praying for more churches to renew their commitment to disciple more families in the Word of God.

If we would reset our lives to the strengthening of families, in just a few short years America would see a harvest of strong families living out their faith for Christ. We pray you will be a part of God's restoration plan for families in America. There are millions of families all over the United States who need to be disciples of the Word of God. America needs you.

Community of the Church

Community is meant to be meaningful. It was essential for survival back in the early days of America because it was a means to support families, form a strong education, build up religion, as well as create jobs and grow the economy.

Reality is that the early Americans had a much better concept of community than we often do today. In fact, we would venture to say that community is a lost art in our culture nowadays. Back then much of the community was built around the church and schoolhouse, but now we identify community to mean Facebook, Twitter, and Instagram, which isn't community at all.

In America's past, community was the overflow of individuality. Christians who lived out their faith united with other like-minded Christians who had a deep concentration of community. From this came communal churches, which became an even bigger overflow of community. Everyone was passionate in sharing community together. It was just a way of life.

This deeply felt community was what made America great. But now look at us. We've lost the need of community. Everybody is off doing their own thing. America has become a nation of zombies, people who are glued to TVs and electronic devices. And what about churches? Where's the community in them? Church is the one place that should be fostering community, and yet most have become a place of disunity.

May God forgive us for this sin, but may we also realize that God will judge the church for neglecting community among its people. The Bible is explicitly clear to all Christians, churches, and denominations in Hebrews 10:24–25: "Consider how to stir up one another to love and good works, not neglecting to meet together, as is the habit of some, but encouraging one another, and all the more as you see the Day drawing near" (ESV).

Community starts with *consideration*. This means that we must consider others before we take care of our own needs. The word *stir* means to provoke or stimulate, which means that we are to be provoked to care for and love others as we stimulate others to do the same. With this purpose in mind, we are not to neglect community in our life. God never intended the Christian life to be lived alone. It may be hard sometimes admitting we have needs, but that is something we need to do. In fact, we all need to invest in the lives of others, and together build a stronger community of like-minded Christians who will reunite this nation that is dying for true and lasting relationships.

STAND STRONG: OBEDIENCE

Before the Pilgrims boldly set sail to America, an ancient Middle Eastern man named Abraham received an earlier revelation to journey to a distant land. This journey embarked on by Abraham would usher in the nation of Israel. Abraham didn't have much to go on—only the words of God, which was more than enough for him to get the job done.

All that was required of Abraham was simple obedience. Abraham "believed the Lord" (Genesis 15:6). And with that bold faith, he "went, not knowing where he was going" (Hebrews 11:8). But as long as God called him and led him, then Abraham had nothing to worry about.

Abraham's life is a testimony. A life of faith. But, more importantly, Abraham's life is a reminder of God's sovereignty over all things. Take heart in knowing that God is in control of your life. Put your faith in Him, and obey His calling for your life.

CHAPTER 3

GOD AND COUNTRY: A TRUE STORY

Those who cannot remember the past are condemned to repeat it.[1]

—GEORGE SANTAYANA

From the sounds of today's skeptics, one might think that America was founded on a strict separation between faith and government, God and country. It is often assumed that America's founders were deists, agnostics, or even atheists. Yet most of the fifty-five original founders who worked on the Constitution were members of Christian churches. And many of them were ordained ministers.

At focus in our culture is often the controversial phrase "separation of church and state." Yet the words *separation, church,* and *state* are not found in the First Amendment or in any other founding document in America's history. The First Amendment simply says, "Congress shall make no law respecting the establishment of religion or prohibiting the free exercise thereof."

From June 7 through September 25, 1789, Congress discussed the intent of the First Amendment. The congressional records from that period reveal that America's leaders did not want in America what they had in Great Britain. They did not want one denomination running the nation, be it Roman Catholic, Anglican, or any other single denomination. Instead they wanted to live by God's principles, not by one denomination's doctrines or dictates.

Our founders were not fighting Christian influence in the government; rather, they were resisting the creation of a state church similar to what had been experienced in England and other nations in Europe. America's founders decided that religious freedom would be built into the Constitution so people could freely choose how to worship.

James Madison wrote the first version of the First Amendment, and its intent to protect religious freedom is clear: "The civil rights of none shall be abridged on account of religious belief or worship, nor shall any national religion be established." The final version of the First Amendment that was adopted by the founders was written by Fisher Ames of Massachusetts, who was a devout Christian, a man who taught that the first and most fundamental textbook to be used in America's schools should simply be the Bible. He wrote the phrase, "Congress shall make no law respecting the establishment of religion or prohibiting the free exercise thereof."[2]

We often hear that America's diversity is our strength. On the one hand, diversity is good in a pluralistic society. As different cultures interact and ideas are exchanged, society moves forward. But on the other hand, some ideas are mutually exclusive. That is to say, they cannot both be true at the same time. For example, Jesus cannot both be the Messiah and not the Messiah. Jesus Himself said that a house divided against itself cannot stand (Mark 3:25). If America's diversity becomes her core value, then the culture will continually be one marked by confusion, as Islam and atheism seek to have Christianity expunged from the public square.

The True Story of "Separation of Church and State"

Thomas Jefferson served as the third president of the United States and is held by many as the champion of a completely secular separation of church and state. Yet Jefferson, and the other Founding Fathers, actually intended for the First Amendment to simply prevent the establishment of a single Christian denomination. In a letter addressed to Benjamin Rush (a signer of the Declaration), Jefferson said that he opposed the efforts of Episcopalians, the Congregationalists, or any other denomination to achieve "the establishment of a particular form of Christianity." Note that Christianity was a given here; the founders only opposed the sweeping influence of one particular denomination.

In fact, the source of the often-quoted phrase "separation of church and state" does not come from a founding American document. Its origin is a letter Thomas Jefferson wrote to some concerned Baptists of Danbury, Connecticut, on November 7, 1801. The Baptists of Danbury were a group that had experienced severe persecution for their faith. So they wrote to Jefferson, concerned over the words in the First Amendment concerning the "free exercise of religion." To them, this suggested that the right to practice religion was a government-granted right rather than a God-granted right. They feared that the implication was that the American government might regulate religious expression in the form of one national Christian denomination.

Jefferson understood their concern. He responded that freedom to practice religion was indeed a God-given right. Furthermore, he noted it was not the place of government to dictate or hinder matters of religion. In his personal reply to the Danbury Baptist Association, Jefferson wrote that there was "a wall of separation between church and state" to insure that the government would not interfere with religious activities. Jefferson carefully chose words that he knew the Danbury Baptists would understand.

His quote about separation was actually a paraphrase of a quote by Reverend Roger Williams, who himself was a Baptist minister. Williams had written concerning "the hedge or wall of separation between the Garden of the church and the wilderness of the world, God hath ever broke down."[3] Jefferson assured his readers that based upon his understanding of the First Amendment, the US government's hands were tied from controlling the affairs of America's Christian churches.

Then and Now

Today, Jefferson's wording of "separation of church and state" is freely quoted without citing the context or purpose of his original letter. Furthermore, the phrase is used without citing the numerous decisions of US courts at all levels that have recognized and affirmed the Christian heritage of the nation. It has become a widely held assumption that the words "separation of church and state" appear in our founding documents, but in fact they do not.

For the nation's first 150 years, the clear understanding was that the First Amendment was written to prevent the establishment of one national Christian denomination. The House of Representatives delivered a report on March 27, 1854, that stated:

> At the time of the adoption of the Constitution and the amendments, the universal sentiment was that Christianity should be encouraged, but not any one sect (or denomination). In this age, there is no substitute for Christianity. ... That was the religion of the Founders of the republic, and they expected it to remain the religion of their descendants.[4]

As we look at the way that Christianity has influenced the development of America, we find that Thomas Jefferson, the supposed champion of those who promote a secular view of American life and practice, offers words of encouragement:

The Christian religion, when divested of the rags in which they [the clergy] have enveloped it, and brought to the original purity and simplicity of its benevolent institutor [Jesus Christ], is a religion of all others, most friendly to liberty, science, and the freest expansion of the human mind.[5]

R. J. Rushdooney, author of *The Nature of the American System*, made a very important observation as well when he wrote:

The concept of a secular state was virtually non-existent in 1776, as well as in 1787 when the Constitution was written, and no less when the Bill of Rights was adopted. To read the Constitution as a charter for a secular state is to misread history, and to misread it radically. The Constitution was designed to perpetuate a Christian order.

The freedom of the First Amendment from federal interference is not from religion, but for religion in the constitutional states.

John Jay, original chief Justice of the Supreme Court, and one of the three primary writers responsible for the Constitution, even said that we should strive to elect Christians for our rulers: "Providence has given to our people the choicest of their rulers, and it is the duty—as well as the privilege and interest—of our Christian nation to select and prefer Christians for their rulers."[6]

Notice that John Jay calls the United States a Christian nation. He saw no conflict, but rather a benefit, in the mixture of religious convictions and public leadership. The authors of the First Amendment never intended for it to be interpreted so as to deny Christians access to either the government or America's schools. As noted by Associate Supreme Court Justice Joseph Story in 1851:

The real object of the First Amendment was not to countenance, much less advance Mohammedanism [Islam], or

Judaism or infidelity, by prostrating Christianity; but …
to prevent any national ecclesiastical establishment which
should give to a hierarchy the exclusive patronage of the
national government.[7]

When Separate Became Separated

It was not until 1947 in the case of *Everson v. Board of Education*
that the US Supreme Court first noted, "The First Amendment has
erected a wall between church and state. That wall must be kept
high and impregnable. We could not approve the slightest breach."[8]
In this case, proposals were in the works related to offering government aid to private religious schools. The decision was made
to separate government funding from religious education, using
Jefferson's quote as a source.

However, this "high and impregnable wall" has continued to
grow since that time. In 1962 and 1963, this same approach was
used to remove public prayer and Bible reading from schools.
Today, actions have been declared using this principle that would
shock our Founding Fathers. The removal of the Ten Commandments from America's courthouses, for example, should simply
point out that those who originally ruled in favor of the practice
had no problem with the Ten Commandments in their courtrooms.

The extreme result of this approach to separation now seeks to
privatize religion as much as possible. For example, a person can
pray to God but should not do so to begin a city council meeting
because it could possibly offend someone. Is this what America's
founders fought for and died to protect, a day when thanking God
would be outlawed because it might offend someone?

When Chief Justice Warren Burger argued for the legitimacy
of one city's nativity scene display in 1984, he wrote, "There is
an unbroken history of official acknowledgement by all three
branches of government of the role of religion in American life. …

The Constitution does not require a complete separation of church and state. It affirmatively mandates accommodation, not merely tolerance, of all religions and forbids hostility to any."[9] Yet today we see open hostility not simply to the true meaning of Christmas but to the very word *Christmas* itself.

This is much more than a separation of church and state as noted by Jefferson. This is more like the ungodly "separate but equal" discrimination that dominated Southern culture for many years. African Americans did not experience a life that was equal in any sense of the word. Today, many Christians experience a similar backlash from opponents. Critics declare separation as "equal," but instead undermine both Christian and American values through removing religious presence in unprecedented ways.

We appreciate the example of President Franklin D. Roosevelt, who, on Christmas Eve, 1944, during the dark days of World War II, stated:

> Here, at home, we will celebrate this Christmas Day in our traditional American way because of its deep spiritual meaning to us; because the teachings of Christ are fundamental in our lives; and because we want our youngest generation to grow up knowing the significance of this tradition and the story of the coming of the immortal Prince of Peace and Good Will.[10]

How is it that we've gone from the words of Roosevelt in 1944 and Burger in 1984 to a society today in which media and merchandisers bend over backward to avoid saying the word *Christmas*? We live in a time when school administrators no longer give students Christmas vacation but winter holidays. The truth is that many love everything about Christmas except Christ. However, America cannot truly enjoy the benefits of Christmas without acknowledging the baby of Christmas—Jesus Christ Himself.

Some secularists in America are actually aiming to make this nation a humanist theocracy with the "god" being the dictates of the state on everything from contraception to same-sex marriage. Our nation was founded on the belief that people must be free to worship God according to the dictates of their conscience. In his famous Virginia Statute on Religious Freedom, Thomas Jefferson, who strongly urged against compelling religious belief, also strongly condemned "the impious presumption of legislators and rulers, civil as well as ecclesiastical, who being themselves but fallible and uninspired men, have assumed dominion over the faith of others, setting up their own opinions and modes of thinking as the only true and infallible, and as such endeavouring to impose them on others."[11]

Jefferson begins by acknowledging almighty God as the creator of all humanity. Unfortunately, what Jefferson feared—ideological tyranny—is what Americans increasingly face today. Christians across this nation are being forced to pay for abortion in violation of their consciences. Not only that, but Christian business owners are fined or sent to sensitivity training for not participating in same-sex marriage ceremonies. This isn't religious freedom at all; this is tyranny.

Make no mistake about it: we're not talking about simple differences in belief styles; we're talking about fundamental contradictions in worldviews. Unless we recognize that true religious freedom, and true freedom of any kind for that matter, can exist only when we believe in the God of the Bible who gave that freedom, our nation will soon cease to be the land of the free that we love so much.

The preservation and future prosperity of our great nation entirely depends on the restoration of the Judeo-Christian worldview to our national consciousness. The only way this is truly going to happen is not through a political renewal but a spiritual revival.

As the First Great Awakening was a precursor to our nation's independence, another great revival can serve as the precursor to the preservation and rebirth of liberty in our land.

A striking example was seen when HGTV canceled plans to air *Flip It Forward*, a house-flipping show set to premier in 2014, because the hosts, twin brothers David Benham and Jason Benham, are strong believers in Christ who stand up for their Christian faith. The network's decision came after RightWingWatch.org, an anticonservative and anti-Christian site, attacked the Benhams for defending life for the unborn and supporting marriage as being between one man and one woman.

I (Alex) have spent time with these two men and have found them as anything but hateful toward others. The Benhams are highly successful entrepreneurs who have built a multimillion-dollar real estate company—they love Jesus and believe the Bible. Yet there is a growing movement in our culture to create a society in which Christians are no longer allowed to voice their opinion. This is not separation of church and state; it is separation of freedom from society, the freedom of religious expression our Founding Fathers sought to provide and protect in the formation of our country.

PRAYING FOR SPIRITUAL AWAKENING

In the early 1900s, 45 percent of the world had heard of Jesus. Thanks to mission movements, revival, and the grace of God, by the year 2000, 70 percent of the world had heard the name of Christ. Christians everywhere need to fast and pray that God would pour out His grace in these dark and difficult days. God is a faithful Father who delights in answering the prayers of His children. We live in a time of great crisis, but within crisis lies opportunity for the advancement of the gospel and God's kingdom.

America became a nation, and then a great nation, not merely because some charismatic leaders got together and decided to declare independence from England. The very roots of our civil order extend into the bedrock of the moral law that originates with God. Acknowledgement of this God, and of the natural law stemming from Him, was requisite to the establishment of America. Our nation didn't emerge from a moral vacuum in which morality is self-determined, with the rule of law optional and God not permitted in the public arena. Our liberties have a source, and eliminating the source of our liberties will unquestionably eliminate the existence of our liberties.

It was renowned American President Abraham Lincoln's observation that "it is the duty of nations … to recognize the sublime truth announced in the Holy Scriptures and proven by all history, that those nations only are blessed, whose God is the Lord."[12] If we truly want to be a great and blessed nation once again, then we need to recognize the truth revealed to us in the Bible, and turn once again to the Lord.

CHAPTER 4

UNCOMMON
COMMON SENSE

From the errors of other nations, let us learn wisdom.[1]
—THOMAS PAINE

The year was 1776, and America had declared its independence from England. The celebration of freedom, however, would have to wait because the American Revolution was underway. Angered by the Declaration of Independence, the king of England sent a heavy fleet of warships filled with redcoats. Their mission was to take back America by all means necessary.

After eight gruesome years, the American Revolution was finally over. Nevertheless, the problems in America grew worse with each passing year. America may have won its freedom from tyranny, but it had yet united the independent unions. The divided unions troubled many of the delegates who represented their states. Even George Washington was concerned.

It was after the war with Britain that George Washington felt the Articles of Confederation were inadequate to advance a growing America. And he wasn't the only one. Though the Confederation Congress tried forming a government of democracy free from intrusion, it still lacked the ability and structure to unite the states. Indeed, the Articles gave representatives of each state the opportunity to voice opinions and establish a way to protect their unions. Even so, in a matter of a few short years, most of the states had rejected the Articles altogether—and even stopped sending their delegates to the Confederate meetings.

By 1786 rebellion had broken out throughout the states, the harshest of them coming out of Massachusetts. A group of farmers went against the enforcement of paying their state and local debts (known today as Shays' Rebellion). But what the riots revealed to the Confederation, as well as to all Americans, was that federalized power was too weak in preventing these and other riots from breaking out.

Desperate to restore peace and order, the Constitutional Convention convened in 1787, the main purpose of which was to find a way to strengthen this feeble government. As you can well imagine, the founders worried that if they couldn't come up with solutions fast enough, the end, at least as they knew it, of the American experiment would not be far behind.

And to think that just a few short years before this, America defended their freedoms by defeating the world's foremost military power during the American Revolution. Yet now a faction of farmers could be America's demise. Nevertheless, the cry for freedom still reigned in the air. Many of the prominent figures leading the newfound nation—men like Benjamin Franklin, John Adams, Thomas Jefferson, and our first president, George Washington— remained resolute in restoring America to order. Their great determination and unrelenting belief in God helped construct the greatest national government the world has ever known.

It was a young, intelligent, and very astute lawyer by the name of Alexander Hamilton who would urge the delegates of the Continental Congress to allow representatives from each of the thirteen colonies to convene a Constitutional Convention in Philadelphia and draft a document fit to restore America. And it was in the rooms of the Constitutional Convention that originated one of the greatest documents ever written: the Constitution of the United States of America.

James Madison and Alexander Hamilton, with some guidance of the "federalists," helped amend the Articles of Confederation. Subsequently, under the leadership of George Washington, the Constitution was ratified and set over the nation in 1788. Through the expressed written words of this new founding document, the founders had created a more perfect union among the states. They created a government with checks and balances, which was a deliberate measure to prevent despotism over the states. But to guarantee and secure individual rights, James Madison would write what is known today as the Bill of Rights.

In 1789, James Madison presented nineteen in all before Congress. By 1791, the first ten amendments of the Bill of Rights were ratified and became part of the Constitution of the United States, which was a historical feat indeed. America had finally achieved not only its independence but also found a way to protect and enrich the freedoms of each and every one of its citizens.

Powerful Truths

The Constitution and the Bill of Rights are certainly two of the greatest achievements in modern civilization. However, most Americans have no clue what's really in them. They may know about their importance, but they may know really nothing beyond that. We need to change this, which is why we encourage you to take time to read the Declaration of Independence, the Constitution, and the Bill of Rights. Get familiar with them. Study them. If you are a parent, get your kids reading these documents. Don't assume they will learn them in school, for the truth is that public schools aren't teaching children the true history about our founding documents, even how America became the United States.

To help you understand our founding documents, we've provided you a simple rundown of some of the common sense found in the Declaration, the Constitution, and the Bill of Rights. Our prayer is that this common sense won't be so uncommon anymore.

Common Sense #1: Certainty in Natural Law

Law. Order. Freedom. Fundamental truths, principles, and rights that come from God—not man—which is a belief strongly held and articulated in the Declaration of Independence, Constitution, and the Bill of Rights. Thomas Jefferson wrote,

> Man has been subjected by his Creator to the moral law, of which his feelings, or conscience as it is sometimes called, are the evidence with which his Creator has furnished him. ... The moral duties which exist between individual and individual in a state of nature, accompany them into a state of society. Their Maker not having released them from those duties on their forming themselves into a nation.[2]

Both the recognition and yielding to natural law revolutionized life as we know it.

Much of history had been dominated and ruled by aristocrats, kings, emperors, and dictators—never *by* the people and *for* the people. However, America's founding documents changed all of that. They looked to a higher law—God's law. His law was a higher order that didn't change. The amazing truth is that these unchanging laws don't apply to a select few; they are meant for all humanity who bear the image of their Creator.

Common Sense #2: Belief in God and the Practice of Religion

Our founders were religious, and each one believed religion was vital to the survival and advancement of America. They believed the government benefited from having a religious people. George

Washington wrote, "While we are zealously performing the duties of good citizens and soldiers, we certainly ought not to be inattentive to the higher duties of religion. To the distinguished character of Patriot, it should be our highest glory to add the more distinguished character of Christian."[3] All people had the right to enjoy and exercise their religious liberties without interference.

The government, both state and federal, did not have the authority to restrict or prevent someone from freely exercising their religion. James Madison, key writer of *The Federalist*, and a major contributor to the ratification of the Constitution and Bill of Rights, said, "We have staked the whole future of American civilization, not upon the power of government, far from it. We've staked the future of all our political institutions upon our capacity … to sustain ourselves according to the Ten Commandments of God."[4]

Common Sense #3: Liberty and Justice for All

The Bill of Rights was an immeasurable leap to protect the rights of every American citizen—rights that guaranteed the security and opportunity to live life to the fullest. Our founders believed strongly in the dignity and equality of each and every person. Everyone—no matter their color, background, education, or religion—has natural rights according to the natural order ordained by God. Our founders believed that inherent rights are a gift of God, and those rights need to be protected at all costs. And that is exactly what they did—sought to protect those rights at all costs.

Common Sense #4: Government Is to Be a Republic, not a Monarchy

Thank God for James Madison and Thomas Jefferson, for if it weren't for these two patriots, the government would be a monarchy, not a republic. Prior to writing the Bill of Rights, Madison had completed the "Virginia Plan," which was a robust national government ideology with checks and balances. It was quite different than what was previously thought up and established.

During the course of many drafts, Thomas Jefferson and James Madison exchanged countless letters. Jefferson voiced the need for rights that were focused on freedom of speech, religion, and the press, protection of habeas corpus laws, trial by jury, and countless other freedoms now expressed in the Bill of Rights. Now that was some common sense!

Another extraordinary piece of common sense from Jefferson was limiting the office of the president. This was seen as a threat to the freedoms of Americans, according to Jefferson. Thankfully, the delegates listened and put in place certain restrictions. All and all, here's some common sense about government from our founders:

- The government is not to have power over the people, but people over the government.
- The government is instituted among people and receives its allotted role to serve and protect them.
- The government is to preserve the unalienable rights of the people.
- The government is to submit to the power of the people if they see the right to dissolve or abolish it and institute a new government.
- The government is not to legislate arbitrary or capricious laws, but only laws that the governed consent.
- The government is to enact justice.
- The government is to regulate commerce between the states and maintain a strong currency.
- And the government is to protect the life, liberty, and property of the people from threats within and abroad.[5]

When you read through these most basic beliefs, the common sense outlined seems to be clear and indisputable. But America has turned away from these common sense beliefs and practices in exchange for practicing a lie. Of course, as we all know, when a nation doesn't seek and follow the laws of God, there will be swift consequences that soon follow. And all of this is having an impact on faith and freedom, to which we'll turn in the following chapter.

STAND STRONG: WISDOM

We are blessed to have a heritage whereby our founders had a lot of wisdom and common sense. No one can ever have enough wisdom. Therefore, make it a top priority to pursue as much wisdom as you can in your daily life. Wisdom will give you the discernment and the knowledge to do the right thing every time. Proverbs 3:13–14 says, "Blessed is the one who finds wisdom, and the one who gets understanding, for the gain from her is better than gain from silver and her profit better than gold" (ESV). The word *finds* means "reaches" or "obtains by seeking." It takes a passionate pursuit to gain wisdom. You don't become wise by doing nothing. In fact, gaining wisdom first requires *seeking* it out.

CHAPTER 5

AMERICA: FREEDOM *OF* RELIGION, NOT FREEDOM *FROM* RELIGION

*Congress shall make no law respecting
an establishment of religion,
or prohibiting the free exercise thereof ...*

—FIRST AMENDMENT

In a September 2015 letter addressed to Superintendent D. C. Machen Jr. of Bossier Parish Schools, the ACLU (American Civil Liberties Union) claimed Airline High School "has engaged in a pattern of religious proselytization by establishing 'prayer boxes' with Christian symbols throughout the school and by religious messages in newsletters posted on the school's website." They added, "This letter is to inform you that these practices violate the First Amendment of the US Constitution and comparable provisions of the Louisiana Constitution, and they must stop immediately." In response, the Airline High School board unanimously ruled against complying with this letter's demands. They pointed out that US history is built on "freedom of religion, not freedom from religion," noting they did not violate the Constitution as alleged.[1]

Unfortunately, such accusations are increasingly made in our nation today. Those who oppose Christian influence continue to work through legal action to harass and change traditional expressions of faith in schools, workplaces, government, and communities in an effort to remove religious expression. In fact, one such organization has chosen this very name: Freedom from Religion Foundation. Its stated purposes are "to promote the constitutional principle of separation of state and church, and to educate the public on matters relating to nontheism."

Some of the Freedom from Religion Foundation's celebrated accomplishments include halting a government chaplaincy to minister to state workers, winning a legal challenge ending fifty-one years of illegal Bible instruction in Rhea County (Dayton, Tennessee) public schools, winning a federal court decision over-turning a law declaring Good Friday a state holiday, and ending commencement prayers at a top ten university.[2] Furthermore, this organization has become known among the public for its letters to public schools and universities to help end public prayers of various types at sporting events and to stop cheerleaders from using banners with Scripture verses on them during athletic events.

Despite these and a growing number of recent challenges to the freedom of religion for Christians, America remains a nation where the words of its first president, George Washington, are upheld: "For you, doubtless, remember that I have often expressed my sentiment, that every man, conducting himself as a good citizen, and being accountable to God alone for his religious opinions, ought to be protected in worshipping the Deity according to the dictates of his own conscience."[3]

The Founding Fathers encouraged the "free exercise" of religion; they did not discourage public expressions of faith. The First Amendment specifically notes, "Congress shall make no law respecting an establishment of religion, or prohibiting the free exercise thereof." Three key observations are inherent in this statement. First, Congress will make "no law." In other words, the government is not to be involved in forcing religion of one kind over another through legislation.

Second, this prohibition is related directly to the "establishment of religion." Does a box at a school that accepts prayer requests "establish" or set up a religion in a school? Of course it doesn't. Instead, it offers a service to assist students who wish to use it. As long as this activity is voluntary, it is not establishing a religion, and thus doesn't violate the First Amendment.

Third, the First Amendment includes not "prohibiting the *free exercise* thereof." In other words, it includes not only choice of one's religion, but also the expression of one's religious convictions. Why is this important? According to the First Amendment Center, "Without the First Amendment, religious minorities could be persecuted, the government might well establish a national religion, protesters could be silenced, the press could not criticize government, and citizens could not mobilize for social change."[4]

If we ever forget that we are One Nation Under God, then we will be a nation gone under.[5]

—*Ronald Reagan*

America's Declaration of Independence also notes the importance of religious freedom, stating, "We hold these truths to be self-evident: That all men are created equal; that they are endowed by their Creator with certain unalienable rights; that among these are life, liberty, and the pursuit of happiness; that, to secure these rights, governments are instituted among men, deriving their just powers from the consent of the governed." Acknowledging both a Creator and the freedoms the Creator offers, the Declaration of Independence has stood for both personal and religious freedom since the earliest days of the United States.

The US Constitution also explicitly states, "No religious Test shall ever be required as a Qualification of any Office or public Trust under the United States." Rather than requiring those holding public office to be affiliated with a particular religion or any religion at all, the Constitution provides ample freedom of religion for its governing leaders. Yet those who oppose Christian influence in society often take the extreme approach that attempts to remove all religious symbolism and traditions from public life. Those caught in the crossfires of such attacks must stand their ground, remembering our nation's conviction is freedom *of* religion, not freedom *from* religion. A look at our nation's founders helps to support this view.

The Origins of America's Religious Freedoms

The Mayflower Compact, the first governmental document adopted by the Pilgrims, was signed and agreed upon on November 11, 1620, before the Pilgrims disembarked from the *Mayflower*. This compact was our first document of self-government and influenced the other founding documents. The settlers clearly stated their intent: "We, whose names are underwritten, having undertaken *for the glory of God, and the advancement of the Christian faith ...*" (emphasis added). Their two-fold purpose was clearly stated: the Pilgrims emphasized living to display God's glory and to advance the Christian faith. The founding of America would continue to reinforce these convictions for generations to come.

The Bible at the Core of American Thought and Life

Political science professors at the University of Houston examined 15,000 writings from the founding era of American history. Their intent was to "rightfully determine the source of the Founders' ideas, and to see whom the Founders quoted." They isolated

3,154 direct verbatim quotes from the founders, and identified the sources of the quotes. They observed that

- 34 percent of founders' quotes came directly from the Bible—verbatim;
- 8.3 percent came from Baron Charles de Montesquieu;
- 7.9 percent came from Sir William Blackstone; and
- 2.9 percent came from John Locke.

The Bible was quoted four times more than Montesquieu, four times more than Blackstone, and twelve times more than Locke. Furthermore, many of the popular sources in this study relied heavily on the Bible for their content. While 34 percent of the founders' quotes included direct quotations of Scripture, even the other influences were often from the writings of men who were also directly influenced by the sixty-six books of the Bible.

George Washington

Such influence certainly connects with the high view of the Bible and of Christianity that was held among early American leaders. For example, our first US president, George Washington, noted, "It is impossible to rightly govern the world without the Bible."[6] Washington was known as a devout Christian, and he let his witness for Christ show in both actions and words. He kept a handwritten journal of his personal prayers and reflections, which he entitled "Daily Sacrifice." When this book was sold at auction in 1891, it was discovered that many of these intimate and personal prayers were written when he was about twenty years old. They reflect deep insights for a young adult, and it was known that George Washington prayed these prayers twice daily, each day of the week, for most of his life.

The twenty-four-page notebook contains many sentiments like the following:

Almighty God, most merciful Father,
who didst command the children of Israel to offer up a daily
    sacrifice to Thee;
that they thereby might glorify and praise Thee for Thy protection both night and day;
receive, O Lord, my morning sacrifice which I now offer up
    to Thee;
… accept me for the merits of Thy Son Jesus Christ,
that when I come into Thy Temple,
and compass Thy altar,
my prayers may come before Thee as incense;
O most glorious God, in Jesus my merciful and loving Father,
… I have called upon Thee for pardon and forgiveness of sins,
    but so coldly and carelessly,
that my prayers are become my sin and stand in need of pardon.
… Increase my faith, and direct me to the true object,
Jesus Christ, the Way, the Truth, and the Life.
Bless O Lord, the people of this land.[7]

This prayer, along with several others, were offered up and written down by America's first president, noting the important role of
faith and Scripture in the nation's founding.

Benjamin Franklin

Benjamin Franklin, the American statesman, author, scientist,
and inventor, was largely self-educated. Franklin taught himself five languages and became envoy to France and England.
He served as governor of Pennsylvania, and was a signer of the
Declaration of Independence, the Articles of Confederation, and
the US Constitution. Many do not realize he also organized the
US postal system, America's first fire department, and a public
library.

On Thursday, June 28, 1787, Benjamin Franklin addressed the Constitutional Convention and requested that each day's session begin with prayer. During the speech, he famously remarked, "The longer I live, the more convincing proofs I see of this Truth—that God governs in the Affairs of Men."[8] How does an alleged deist, someone who believes that God created the universe but allows it to function merely through natural laws, believe that God governs the affairs of men?

Benjamin Franklin founded the Pennsylvania Hospital in 1751, and when a permanent building was built several years later, he composed the words for the cornerstone:

In the year of Christ, 1755. This building was piously founded, for the relief of the sick and miserable.
May the God of mercies bless the undertaking.
Whoever shall introduce into public affairs the principles of primitive Christianity will change the face of the world.

Known for his hard work and dedication, he was quoted as writing, "Work as if you were to live 100 years; pray as if you were to die tomorrow."[9]

Patrick Henry

Patrick Henry served as governor of Virginia, was a leader in the American Revolution, and spoke the famous phrase, "Give me liberty, or give me death!" He noted, "The Bible is worth all other books which have ever been printed."[10] Patrick Henry was among those who, in 1784, worked for a law establishing "Provision for Teachers of the Christian Religion." It did not occur to Henry and the other Founders that this would somehow violate the First Amendment (which it wouldn't). They understood what many today do not—that the promotion of moral law (natural law) does not violate the "Establishment clause" of the First Amendment. Preserving moral boundaries (civility) is not a form of religion (ceremony) and would promote the general welfare of the people. As Henry stated, "The general diffusion of Christian knowledge hath a natural tendency to correct the morals of men, restrain their vices, and preserve the peace of society."[11] Henry clearly believed that the public's instruction in Christian teaching was essential to America's moral fabric and future.

John Adams

John Adams served as the second president of our country and was the first to live in the White House. He established the Library of Congress, the US Navy, authored the Constitution of Massachusetts, and personally encouraged Thomas Jefferson to write the Declaration of Independence. He also wrote:

> The general principles on which the fathers achieved independence were...the general principles of Christianity. ... Now I will avow, that I then believed, and now believe that those general principles of Christianity are as eternal and immutable as the existence and attributes of God.[12]

In another document, John Adams later shared, "Our constitution was made only for a moral and religious people. It is wholly inadequate to the government of any other."[13]

Thomas Jefferson

Regarding the nation's founders and their intended role for religion to play in American life, few topics have drummed up as much related discussion as the subject of Thomas Jefferson's beliefs. Thomas Jefferson served as the third president of our nation. Admittedly, determining his religious beliefs is a complicated subject. But having devoted nearly twenty years of research to this subject, I (Alex) have come to three definite conclusions:

1. The general public is largely clueless on this matter—and never more so than when they mindlessly pass along sound-bite assertions of Jefferson's secularism, which they learned in public school or read on a blog site.

2. Even those evangelical patriots who actually do care about the role of Christianity in American life have largely "thrown in the towel" on defending Jefferson's religious convictions. Nowadays, Jefferson is routinely depicted as a deist, secularist, and/or libertine who would happily side with the platforms of the left. Christians don't raise much of a peep when this caricature is presented. In fact, many are complicit with this portrayal.

3. Jefferson's religious beliefs changed (vacillated) throughout different periods of his life. There were a host of mitigating factors that contributed to his changes of belief, including the death of his wife and the lengthy depression that followed him for years afterward, financial pressures that dogged him for much of his adult life, and the likely influence of French Enlightenment thinkers such as Pierre Cabanas (with whom Jefferson was acquainted during his years representing the US while living in Paris). Jefferson's statements about Christianity can only begin to be understood by also considering the context of his life during which his many statements were made. Any conclusions made about Jefferson's thoughts about God, the Bible, Jesus, Christianity, the church, or "organized religion" should really take into consideration the different seasons and circumstances which seem to form an influential backdrop to his expressed religious sentiments.

With all of that in mind, note that in 1779, while Jefferson was the Governor of Virginia, he proclaimed a Day of Prayer, affirming that, "Almighty God … hath diffused the glorious light of the Gospel, whereby, through the merits of our gracious Redeemer, we may become the heirs of His eternal glory."[14] More affirmations consistent with classical Christian orthodoxy are present in statements such as: "Can the liberties of a nation be thought secure when we have removed their only firm basis, a conviction in the minds of the people that these liberties are of the gift of God? That they are not to be violated but with His wrath? Indeed I tremble for my country when I reflect that God is just, and that His justice cannot sleep forever."[15] Jefferson's financial support for more than 150 churches and/or ministers and his initiatives to take Bibles to native Americans are well documented. For more on this, I recommend reading Mark A. Bellies and Jerry Newcombe's *Doubting Thomas? The Religious Life and Legacy of Thomas Jefferson.*[16]

It has also been well documented (perhaps overly so) that Jefferson made remarks unfavorable toward Christianity. For example, he wrote that clergy had "enveloped the Christian religion in rags."[17] Jefferson's words to nephew Peter Carr are also often repeated: "Question with boldness even the existence of a God … keep in your eye those who say, 'He [Jesus] was begotten by God, [and] born of a virgin.'"[18]

As you can see, an accurate understanding of Jefferson's convictions about Christianity requires diligent study and an open mind. Unfortunately, even tragically, this is a pursuit that few people today seem willing to undergo.

Did Jefferson ever have a personal relationship with Jesus Christ? It is possible that he did, though I don't think anyone alive today definitively knows. Benjamin Rush—a devout Christian and fellow signer of the Declaration of Independence—told Jefferson, who was his friend, that Jefferson was "by no means so heterodox as [he had] been supposed by [his] enemies."[19] We would do well to keep that in mind when we consider the convictions of our nation's third president.

Samuel Adams

Samuel Adams was a cousin of John Adams, and he was known as "The Father of the American Revolution." In fact, he was the man who instigated the Boston Tea Party. But he also signed the Declaration of Independence and served as a member of Congress. In his writings, he noted: "The [rights of the colonists as Christians] may be best understood by reading and carefully studying the institutes of the great Law Giver and Head of the Christian Church, which are to be found clearly written and promulgated in the New Testament."[20]

On September 6, 1774, the second day of the Continental Congress, Samuel Adams proposed that the session be opened with prayer. He wrote of the proceedings of the Continental Congress: "Christian men ... [came] together for solemn deliberation in the hour of their extremity."[21] When his cousin John Adams was vice president, he wrote to him, saying:

> Let divines [ministers] and philosophers, statesmen and patriots, unite their endeavors to renovate the age, by impressing the minds of men, with the importance of educating their little boys and girls, of inculcating in the minds of youth the fear and love of the Deity [God] ... in short, of leading them in the study and practice of the exalted virtues of the Christian system.[22]

John Quincy Adams

John Quincy Adams was the son of John Adams, who was America's second president, and he served as America's sixth president. He wrote, "The first and almost the only book deserving

57

of universal attention is the Bible."[23] Many do not know that for many years John Quincy Adams was also a member of the American Bible Society and served as one of its vice presidents. In 1830 he wrote a letter to that body, stating:

> The distribution of Bibles, if the simplest, is not the least efficacious of the means of extending the blessings of the Gospel to the remotest corners of the earth; for the Comforter is in the sacred volume: and among the receivers of that million of copies distributed by the Society, who shall number the multitudes awakened thereby, with good will to man in their hearts, and with the song of the Lamb upon their lips?
>
> The hope of a Christian is inseparable from his faith. Whoever believes in the divine inspiration of the holy Scriptures, must hope that the religion of Jesus shall prevail throughout the earth. Never since the foundation of the world have the prospects of mankind been more encouraging to that hope than they appear to be at the present time. And may the associated distribution of the Bible proceed and prosper, till the Lord shall have made "bare his holy arm in the eyes of all the nations; and all the ends of the earth shall see the salvation of our God."[24]

Andrew Johnson

Andrew Johnson, America's seventeenth president, spoke of the power of the cross of Jesus as being much greater than the concerns of the nation: "Let us look forward to the time when we can take the flag of our country, and nail it below the Cross, and there let it wave as it waved in the olden times, and let us gather around it and inscribe for our motto: 'Liberty and Union, one and inseparable, now and forever,' and exclaim, Christ first, our country next!"[25]

Noah Webster

Noah Webster was an American statesman, educator, soldier, and author of the 1828 edition of *Webster's American Dictionary of the English Language*. A highly devout Christian, he has left many quotes noting the importance of his faith. In his acknowledgement of Christianity to the nation's heritage, he wrote:

> The religion which has introduced civil liberty is the religion of Christ and His apostles … to this we owe our free constitutions of government.
>
> The Christian religion is the most important and one of the first things in which all children, under a free government, ought to be instructed. No truth is more evident to my mind than that the Christian religion must be the basis of any government intended to secure the rights and privileges of a free people.[26]

Webster also called the Bible America's basic textbook in all fields and claimed education was useless without it.

Abraham Lincoln

Abraham Lincoln served as the sixteenth president of the United States and was leader of our nation during the tumultuous time of the Civil War. During these difficult times, he shared, "It is announced in the Holy Scriptures and proven by all history, that those nations are blessed whose God is the Lord."[27]

Grover Cleveland

Twenty-second US President Grover Cleveland, on the occasion of his first inauguration (March 4, 1885), said, "Let us not trust to human effort alone, but humbly acknowledge the power and goodness of Almighty God who presides over the destiny of nations, and who has at all times been revealed in our country's history, let us invoke His aid and His blessings upon our labors."[28]

Woodrow Wilson

As the twenty-eighth president of the United States, Woodrow Wilson continued to uphold the importance of the Bible in American life. When speaking of Scripture, he wrote, "The Bible is the one supreme source of revelation of the meaning of life."[29] He also stated, "When you have read the Bible you will know that it is the Word of God, because you will have found it the key to your own heart, your own happiness, and your own duty."[30]

Religious Freedom Today

Some American leaders continue this tradition of supporting freedom of religion today, regardless of whether or not it is popular in our culture. For example, Louisiana governor Bobby Jindal said in a recent interview, "Without religious liberty rights, there would be no freedom of speech. ... America did not create religious liberty; religious liberty created America."[31]

This speech arose regarding his effort to provide religious freedom for those who choose not to participate in same-sex marriage ceremonies or services due to their religious beliefs. While his words merely echo the beliefs of our nation's founders, there are many who now oppose such freedoms when they do not support their particular worldview or practices.

> Does the Bible really teach that homosexuality is sinful? Wasn't that just a law in Leviticus that applied to the people of Israel? After all, Jesus never explicitly said anything about homosexuality. We often hear such conversation today, yet we cannot say that something is not sinful simply because Jesus didn't teach directly on the subject. Jesus never condemned rape, yet we can be sure that rape is sinful. Moreover, while Jesus never directly taught against homosexuality, He did give us a picture of what God intended marriage to be, even from the beginning of creation (Matthew 19:4–6).

In order for our nation to stand strong, men and women of conviction must be willing to stand for religious freedom and "the free exercise thereof" when it is convenient and when it is not. When we do this, we may find a struggle on our hands, yet we'll also find ourselves working to support the same themes our nation's Founding Fathers pursued that made our country great.

How can we hope to see God at work in our lives and our nation? It is not through our own strength, but through the power of the Holy Spirit. He is not a mere force that influences us. As the third person of the triune God, the Holy Spirit is eternal (Hebrews 9:14), omnipresent (Psalm 139:7), and omniscient (1 Corinthians 2:10). He is a creator (Psalm 104:30) who acts in power (1 Corinthians 12:11), gives life (Romans 8:10–11), and strengthens believers (Ephesians 3:16).

A. W. Tozer, a Christian leader who died in the 1960s, wrote, "If the Holy Spirit was withdrawn from the church today, 95 percent of what we do would go on and no one would know the difference. If the Holy Spirit had been withdrawn from the New Testament church, 95 percent of what they did would stop, and everybody would know the difference."[32] The Holy Spirit serves as the key to the current famine in the family and in the church.

> Complementarianism is the idea that men and women are equal in worth and value, and yet complement one another in their functions and roles. In Christianity this plays itself out in several ways. For example, men are to lead their wives, and women are to submit to the leadership of their husbands. This submission does not in any way demean the wife, as the man is to lead her in a loving, respectful manner as Christ leads His church—his role expects him to go as far as to give up his life for his wife.

Finally, the course of our nation is based upon the lives of the individual members of each family. If we wish to change our nation, it must begin with a passionate pursuit of the Lord in our own lives. Let's call out to Him today. James wrote, "Therefore submit to God. Resist the devil and he will flee from you. Draw near to God and He will draw near to you" (4:7–8 NKJV). This promise is true for your life, the lives of those in your family, and the hearts of those across our nation who long to see God at work in them.

CHAPTER 6

AMERICA IS DYING: THREATS FROM WITHIN

Guard against the impostures
of pretended patriotism.[1]
—GEORGE WASHINGTON

By all indications, America is dying. This is not something new. In fact, the deadly symptoms started sometime ago. It seemed, at first, that America was just really sick. But for the past few decades, America's health has been in decline. Its symptoms have progressed into something much worse than what we've ever seen before.

Various opinions about the condition of America have been given and countless treatments recommended. But as time went on, nothing seemed to work. America only got worse. And for whatever reason, our presidents, members of Congress, SCOTUS justices, and other high-profile officials have ignored America's poor condition and kept right on subjecting her to even more threatening ailments. The great Mark Levine writes, "The ruling generation's governing policies are already forecast to diminish the quality of life of future generations."[2]

Well, that's good to know. But is anyone paying attention?

Our leaders think America will get better by treating her with more government bureaucracy. But this is precisely the problem. Instead of removing all the bad things from within America, our elected officials keep feeding our nation with more greed, lust, crime, and deception. David Kupelian, in *The Snapping of the American Mind*, writes:

> Compared with the shining and vibrant nation it once was, today's America has become a different country: deeply and angrily divided, unable to deal with crises foreign or domestic, the world's greatest debtor nation with 50 million people on food stamps, rampant divorce and family breakdown, unprecedented sexual anarchy with 110 million with STDs, almost 60 million abusing alcohol, and over 70 million taking mood-altering drugs.[3]

America is being led with the belief that she's getting better, not worse; that with more indulgence, tolerance, and total reform, she'll be better than ever before. But this carelessness and lack of common sense is what has caused America to become terminally ill.

This way of living without God has produced only despair, debt, and a rather quick death. Bound by extreme sin, America has become a slave to its own desires. A great mentor and friend, Dr. Ravi Zacharias, lays out a telling way of how we got here:

> In the 1950s kids lost their innocence. They were liberated from their parents by well-paying jobs, cars, and lyrics in music that gave rise to a new term—the generation gap.
>
> In the 1960s, kids lost their authority. It was a decade of protest—church, state, and parents were all called into question and found wanting. Their authority was rejected, yet nothing ever replaced it.
>
> In the 1970s, kids lost their love. It was the decade of me-ism dominated by hyphenated words beginning with self.

Self-image, Self-esteem, Self-assertion. … It made for a lonely world. Kids learned everything there was to know about sex and forgot everything there was to know about love, and no one had the nerve to tell them there was a difference.

In the 1980s, kids lost their hope. Stripped of innocence, authority and love and plagued by the horror of a nuclear nightmare, large and growing numbers of this generation stopped believing in the future.

In the 1990s kids lost their power to reason. Less and less were they taught the very basics of language, truth, and logic and they grew up with the irrationality of a postmodern world.

In the new millennium, kids woke up and found out that somewhere in the midst of all this change, they had lost their imagination. Violence and perversion entertained them till none could talk of killing innocents since none was innocent anymore.[4]

Take note of the progression that has taken place here. America went from losing her innocence to losing authority, to losing love, to losing hope, to losing reason, and, finally, to losing her imagination.

Tragically, America went from a nation of great faith to a nation denying such faith. There's no denying that there's still a large population of Christians in America today. But many lack the fervor and determination to live out their faith like Christians did in the past. Best-selling author Paul Kengor writes:

America has entered a protracted phase of post-Christian thinking and ethics, a dismal state where individualism and a dictatorship of relativism reign supreme, fostered by a long line of incredibly naïve parents who marched their children in wide-eyed cadence through the educational system at giant costs both financial and moral. Nothing but a religious revival will save it.[5]

And Mr. Kengor is right. If we're going to save America from coming destruction, then it's going to take real Christians living out their faith *for real*. But there are threats that need to be brought to the attention of millions of Americans; threats within and outside the walls of America. The longer these threats go unnoticed, the more havoc they will have on religious freedom, national security, and the economy. Therefore, it is imperative that Americans wake up to these real-life threats, and muster enough strength to do something about it before it's too late.

Real Threats

Threats are everywhere. In fact, they come in all shapes and sizes. There are death threats, cyber threats, and national security threats. There are health threats, and even threats to the vitality of marriage and the family. However, not all threats are easily detected, especially if they're not perceived as a threat at all.

I (Jason) remember the HOA alerting my neighborhood of some recent car break-ins. One night my neighbor forgot to bring inside his valuables and lock his car doors. The next morning, he awoke to a bombshell—his car was broken into. The perpetrators got away with a load of cash and scored his son's game device. That break-in was definitely real to my neighbor, as it was for me. The threat assessment was real, and it got our attention. From that moment on, I made sure all car doors were locked and all valuables were brought inside every evening.

Maybe you've had a car, office, or house broken into. To be sure, it is not fun. And it can be awfully scary too. But there are certain threats deadlier than a break-in. These threats we speak of are not ones that occur from outside the walls; rather, they come from within the walls. What are these threats we are referring to? They are apathy, ignorance, and deluded narcissism.

These key threats seemingly go undetected. They are presently destroying marriages, families, and churches. Ultimately, apathy, ignorance, and narcissism have become symptomatic to most of the problems facing our nation today. Let's take a brief look at each of these in more detail.

Apathy

Several years ago, the Christian pollster George Barna was speaking to a group of journalists, and what he said was both shocking and profound. He said to the audience, "The enemy of America today is not Iraq. It is not Afghanistan or communism. It is not Somalian pirates. It's the moral degradation and spiritual complacency of Americans. In essence, it is the willingness of Americans to become victims of the imposition of values and objectives that defy our common good."[6]

Just keep in mind, if you ever need a slightly apathetic tertiary friend, I stand at the ready.[7]

—*Dr. Sheldon Cooper,* The Big Bang Theory

Did you catch what Barna said? He said that America is plagued with apathetic citizens who are too complacent to even care about moral or spiritual matters. It seems Americans are aware we got some major problems; yet rather than do something about them, we would much rather sit around and blame institutions like the government and the church.

But why? It is because we've become apathetic. Americans simply lack interest. They're just not that concerned with affairs that don't directly have to do with their daily routines. We would much rather play on our devices and watch our favorite shows than lift a finger to help bring real change. Entertainment options are what interest us. And not complaining isn't entertaining. Giving up on having the latest and greatest isn't any fun. Being proactive takes too much time and requires hard work.

A direct and visible correlation of apathy is the upsurge of obese Americans today. Obesity has gotten so bad in the US that it costs almost $200 billion a year in weight-related medical bills. That's outrageous! But as long as apathy remains, obesity will continue to shorten the lifespan of Americans.

Moreover, apathy is what prevents over half of Americans from voting in presidential elections. In 2012, an estimated 93 million eligible voters didn't even care to vote. It's apathy that prevents 80 percent of Christians from serving in their church, and it is apathy that has driven America to sixth place as the most obese nation in the world. This is simply despicable.

Americans have got to wake up. We have got to stop living like zombies and do something about the current status of our lives and our nation. We spend too much time checking the number of "likes" we get on Facebook that we become too complacent to care about anything of real substance and meaning. Albert Einstein once said, "The world will not be destroyed by those who do evil, but by those who watch them without doing anything."[8]

Americans are quick to complain and blame, but not quick to do anything about it. Instead of becoming proactive, many Americans would rather toss the responsibility to someone else. The problem with this kind of treatment, however, is that nothing ever gets done. We have come to believe that *someone else* will do the heavy lifting, so it doesn't really matter. But it does matter. And we need to wake up out of our slumber and start doing something about it. Passing off problems to someone else is what's gotten America in its current mess.

As a matter of fact, the incompetency among our politicians and religious leaders is precisely due to the apathy plaguing our citizens. If apathy has had a stronghold on your life, we plead with you to ask God to release it from your life. Pray for the willpower to overcome apathy with action.

In Romans 12, Paul offers some powerful ways to actively perform spiritual service to others. He writes,

> Let love be genuine. Abhor what is evil; hold fast to what is good. Love one another with brotherly affection. Outdo one another in showing honor. Do not be slothful in zeal, be fervent in spirit, serve the Lord. Rejoice in hope, be patient in tribulation, be constant in prayer. Contribute to the needs of the saints and seek to show hospitality. (Romans 12:9–13 ESV)

Apathetic people are indifferent to anything and everything happening around them. They show no signs of caring and sharing. They are basically dead to the world. But if more people lived out Romans 12, it would drive them out of apathy and into an active life of total transformation. So we plead with you to ask yourself: How do I want to be remembered? Do I want my family to remember me as apathetic? Or do I want my loved ones to remember me as a person who served the needs of others?

Ignorance

A champion of the faith, and a good friend to both of us, is Todd Starnes of Fox News. We were hosting one of our Truth for a New Generation conferences in Spartanburg, South Carolina, some time ago. In his talk during this particular conference, Starnes told the crowd to stop blaming liberals for making bad policies and stripping religious people of their rights. He reminded the crowd that we, as Christians, are as much to blame for the bad policies as the liberal progressives.

His proof? It all boiled down to Christians being ignorant of their role in society today. And, as such, Christians don't research the issues, study the candidates, educate their families and friends, and, for the most part, don't bother to vote on election day.

To make his point, Todd gave a particular example. He cited how the liberal-lesbian mayor of Houston, Annise Parker, got into office in a very conservative town. How did she do it? Well, the reality is that she really didn't do anything at all. Annise Parker became mayor because only about 13 percent of the people of Houston came out to vote. Translation: one of the most conservative cities in America got a liberal mayor because Christians (and other conservatives) didn't bother showing up to the polls. That's saying something, especially when you consider all the megachurches in Houston. There's practically one on every corner. So what gives?

The bottom line is that Christians are ignorant. Or a nicer way to put it is that Christians don't know any better. They prefer to stay out of American politics and let others run and decide the fate of America. We have pastors today who are too scared to even mention the word *politics* on a Sunday morning. We have churches and pastors more concerned with polling their own numbers, than they are getting large numbers of Christians out to the polls. And the result is that Christians absent at the polls makes their views and values absent in the culture.

Oh, and by the way, after a few short years, Mayor Parker subpoenaed five pastors, demanding they not only hand over their sermons, but their e-mails as well—even their text messages. Her reasoning? She invoked the Nondiscrimination Ordinance (which allows a man who's dressed like a woman or thinks he's a woman to use the woman's bathroom, and vice versa) as a means to use the local government to review their religious and private material to determine if any of these pastors violated the Nondiscrimination Ordinance.

Thankfully, Mr. Erik Stanley came to the rescue, an attorney with Alliance Defending Freedom, and challenged the subpoenas.

He stated, "The entire nation—voices from every point of the spectrum left to right—recognize the city's action as a gross abuse of power. We are gratified that the First Amendment rights of the pastors have triumphed over government overreach and intimidation. The First Amendment protects the right of pastors to be free from government intimidation and coercion of this sort."[9]

Can you imagine? A mayor in America abusing her power and intruding into the affairs of clergy? Well, that is exactly what happened. And it doesn't look like this sort of intrusion will end anytime soon. Todd Starnes is right: this situation (along with others) could have been avoided if Christians stayed informed and stayed active in local politics.

There was once a time when it was Christians who stood up for what was constitutionally right, it was Christians coming to people's aid to protect and defend their freedoms, and it was Christians who ran for public office. Lest we forget, but out of the fifty-five signers of the Constitution, most of them were Christians. Sadly, most Christians today are just too busy and too naïve to even care about the things of God and consider the great things He's done for the United States.

The founders knew it would be next to impossible to advance American life and freedom in the midst of ignorance. Ignorance was something they feared. They knew the day would come when the majority of Americans would disengage in the affairs of their country, which is why John Adams vented, "Liberty cannot be preserved without a general knowledge among the people."[10]

Let's face it. Given all the ignorant leaders we have running the United States, it would take an act of God to turn things around. But if we are serious about God restoring our nation, we first need to get serious about getting right with Him. America doesn't need more *ignorance*; America needs a big dosage of *repentance*.

Americans all across the country need to fall flat on our faces, repenting of our sins, and turning back to God. In 2 Chronicles 7:14, God graciously gives His people a framework of what to do: "If my people who are called by my name humble themselves, and pray and seek my face and turn from their wicked ways, then I will hear from heaven and will forgive their sin and heal their land." The key is *if*. If America subjects herself before God, and returns to Him, then, and only then, will God hear our nation's prayers, forgive our sins, and begin to restore our land. God declares, "I love those who love me, and those who seek me diligently find me" (Proverbs 8:17 ESV).

Yet repentance isn't enough. America needs to regain her hunger and thirst to know God, and, without reservation, to follow after Him. Proverbs 2:5 says, "Then you will understand what it means to fear the LORD, and you will gain knowledge of God" (NLT). We need to pray that America repents of her wicked sins. But as we do so, we need to pray that America will come to fear God once again. David writes, "Who is the man who fears the LORD? Him will he instruct in the way that he should choose" (Psalm 25:12 ESV).

We say this with all respect: Christians who don't vote are really a vote for candidates who will undermine religious freedom, advance abortion, and everything else that runs contrary to the Bible. Calvin Coolidge, the thirteenth president of the United States, said, "If the people fail to vote, a government will be developed which is not their government. … The whole system of American Government rests on the ballot box. Unless citizens perform their duties there, such a system of government is doomed to failure."[11]

We need millions more evangelical Christians to register to vote (details are in the back of this book), but we also need those evangelical Christians who are eligible to vote to actually go out and vote when the time comes. Remaining ignorant, and therefore not voting at all, has severely threatened our freedoms. And if Christians don't start voting for candidates with biblical values, or start running for office themselves, then we can say good-bye to our most treasured freedoms.

We wish this wasn't the case, but sadly it is. So we beg you, please pray. Pray that the ignorance among evangelical Christians will be turned into substance and action. Benjamin Franklin was right when he said, "The only thing more expensive than education is ignorance."[12] Look around. Many of the problems you see, read, and hear about are the price America is paying because of ignorant Americans. And this needs to end.

To see this ignorance end, it needs to start with you. It starts by what you are doing right now, even by you taking the time to read what we have written. But make sure you take what you learn from this book and help inform your family, friends, and your church. In fact, we are praying for more Christians just like you. That you, and your sphere of influence, will all become the solution to putting an end to the plague of ignorance that blankets our country today.

Deluded Narcissists

Have you ever taken a selfie? If you have taken one, why did you do it? Did you do it to show off your body? To show off your hair? Your wardrobe? Whatever the reason, selfies not only capture a pose in time, but, ironically, they capture the deluded narcissism (an obsession with self) that has permeated the culture in which we live.

We are living in a time when the majority of young people think more highly of themselves than they ought to think. There is a growing obsession among Americans that the world needs to know how extremely gifted and talented we are. All we have to do is watch *American Idol, The Voice,* and *America's Got Talent.* Many of the participants have some talent, but most of them think their talent is better than it really is. They think, *I'll just kill it on stage in front of millions watching and become an instant star!*

Dr. Keith Ablow, a psychiatrist and member of the Fox News Medical A-Team, explains this obsession as "faux celebrities," which is the equivalent of young people believing they are the lead role in their own fictionalized story.[13] This generation has grown up with social media platforms that cater to and feed on their pride, self-centeredness, and passions, and they have come to believe that life is all about them. And life will be so much better if people would just recognize how awesome they are.

Dr. Ablow brings the problem of narcissism to light:

Using Twitter, young people can pretend they are worth "following," as though they have real-life fans, when all that is really happening is the mutual fanning of false love and false fame. Using computer games, our sons and daughters can pretend they are Olympians, Formula 1 drivers, rock stars or sharpshooters. And while they can turn off their Wii and Xbox machines and remember they are really in dens and playrooms on side streets and in triple deckers around America, that is after their hearts have raced and heads have swelled with false pride for "being" something they are not. ... These are the psychological drugs of the 21st Century and they are getting our sons and daughters very sick, indeed. As if to keep up with the unreality of media and technology, in a dizzying paroxysm of self-aggrandizing hype, town sports leagues across the country hand out ribbons and trophies to losing teams, schools inflate grades, energy drinks in giant, colorful cans take over the soft drink market, and psychiatrists hand out Adderall like candy. All the while, these adolescents, teens and young adults are watching a Congress that can't control its manic, euphoric, narcissistic spending, a president that can't see his way through to applauding genuine and extraordinary achievements in business, a society that blames mass killings on guns, not the psychotic people who wield them.[14]

This is heartbreaking to hear. But even more troubling is that Americans are trending to become the most narcissistic of all people, which means that narcissism will have an even greater and more devastating effect on society.

Dr. John Townsend is a well-respected author and counselor with a wealth of knowledge. In *The Entitlement Cure*, Dr. Townsend provides a list of how narcissism (or people with a sense of entitlement) has negatively impacted pretty much every aspect of life:

1. Companies that must deal with unmotivated employees.
2. Parents are faced with raising self-centered children.
3. Dating relationships don't work because of an "I'm special, and I deserve more than you're giving me" attitude.
4. Young adults refuse to grow up and so go nowhere.
5. Leaders expect special treatment because of their position, not because of their character.
6. Marriages are torn apart by the narcissism of a spouse.
7. Ministries are saddled with prima donna leadership.
8. Professionals wander from job to job looking for a place that will see them as the wunderkind they consider themselves to be—whether they're productive or not.[15]

There's no denying it: narcissism is a serious problem in America.

To know that every facet of life is being negatively impacted by narcissists makes things seem hopeless. Paul warned Timothy of this very thing:

But understand this, that in the last days there will come times of difficulty. For people will be lovers of self, lovers of money, proud, arrogant, abusive, disobedient to their parents, ungrateful, unholy, heartless, unappeasable, slanderous, without self-control, brutal, not loving good, treacherous, reckless, swollen with conceit, lovers of pleasure rather than lovers of God, having the appearance of godliness, but denying its power. (2 Timothy 3:1–4 ESV)

> Seventy percent of students today score higher on narcissism and lower on empathy than did the average student thirty years ago.[16]

America went from being the most caring and considerate nation to the most self-absorbed and thoughtless nation. This wasn't always the case. But as more people promote logos and flaunt egos, the more empathetic and indifferent they become toward others. Narcissistic people are self-seekers (Philippians 2:21), and, as such, they pay no attention and show little appreciation of the things of Jesus Christ. Narcissistic people are a danger to themselves, to families, churches, and society as a whole.

To hit this threat head on and prevent it from spreading, we need to lay aside our selfish ambitions and conceit, and in "humility count others more significant" than ourselves (Philippians 2:3 ESV). A powerful word of truth to this generation comes from 1 Peter 5:5–6: "Likewise, you who are younger, be subject to the elders. Clothe yourselves, all of you, with humility toward one another, for 'God opposes the proud but gives grace to the humble.' Humble yourselves, therefore, under the mighty hand of God so that at the proper time he may exalt you" (ESV).

We need to pray that America is humbled. We are not sure what that will take and how much of it we need, but we all know that as a nation we are producing and promoting too many *selfie* people, and not enough disciples of Christ. Simply put, we need to get back to putting the needs of others above our own.

Now that you have gotten a bit more insight into the "inside" threats that are destroying America (apathy, ignorance, and narcissism), we now turn to a few "outside" threats that are contributing factors to the crumbling of America today. These outside threats consist of the "Gay Revolution," the growing threat of ISIS, the rise of militant secularism, and the crippling foreign relations with Israel for the backing of Iran.

CHAPTER 7

AMERICA IS UNDER ATTACK: FOUR THREATS FROM BEYOND

The effort to force Christians to violate their consciences must be opposed with all vigor, regardless of the consequences—primarily because it is unconstitutional.[1]

—Dr. James Dobson

The Gay Revolution

In contemporary news, Kim Davis, a county clerk in Kentucky, was unwilling to issue same-sex marriage licenses because it violated her religious convictions, which was something clearly articulated by our founders and protected under the First Amendment. However, since the ruling in June 2015 by the Supreme Court declaring same-sex marriage to be legal, a federal judge had Kim arrested for not complying to the law (never mind he undermined her constitutional rights—but hey, who cares about that, right?). Yet thankfully, Kim only spent a few days locked up in jail.

But unless we're mistaken, this is a serious issue indeed. We find our country at a place in time, where we, as a *free* nation, are permitting judges to revoke people's rights just because they can.

America is now walking down the path where peoples' religious freedoms no longer matter.

Since this clerk controversy, many in the "Gay Mafia" have sent sadistic threats to Kim and her husband. Many of the threats they received are about burning their house down while they sleep. Now ask yourself, does this sound like tolerance? Is this what we've become? Threatening to kill those who oppose same-sex marriage? Seriously?

Kim was only standing up for what she believed in, which is the belief that God ordained marriage to be between one man and one woman. This is a belief embraced and practiced by an over-whelmingly majority of people in history. When asked about why she wouldn't issue same-sex marriage licenses, she declared that it was against God's laws. Kim wasn't forcing her religious beliefs on anyone, she was only staying true to her convictions.

At no point at any time did Kim ever demand the arrest, torture, or execution of homosexuals. She wasn't seeking ways to destroy same-sex couples. She was simply standing on her religious convictions, which is a thing every American (gay or straight) has a right to do.

No person has a right to threaten, rape, sodomize, or kill people who respectfully disagree with them. But this is what we fear has come. The Gay Mafia has taken to social media and to the streets. They are spouting hateful and vile things to those who respectfully disagree with their points of view. It's not the Muslim bakers that the Gay Mafia is targeting; it's the Christian-owned-and-operated businesses they are going after. Yet those Christian owners who refuse to cater or bake a cake for a same-sex wedding are often sued. They are fined, threatened, and assaulted—forcing most to close their doors for good. This is far beyond the indoctrination of the homosexual lifestyle. This is now a hostile takeover of any and all disenchanters of homosexuality.

Gaystapo: Our Lifestyle Wins

The Gay Mafia has become successful in shutting the doors of businesses and organizations that oppose their agenda. Through the years, homosexuals have learned, studied, and stayed true to growing their cause. They have gone from closet dwellers to public promoters; they went from no marriages to nationwide same-sex marriages. And they've accomplished this in less than fifty years.

The gay agenda went from total rejection to awkwardness, awkwardness turned to therapy, and then therapy turned to tolerance. Tolerance turned to acceptance, and now acceptance has turned into celebration. Not only that, but celebration turned to indoctrination, and then indoctrination turned to domination. Now domination is here, and it's here to stay.

Here's a little candid truth behind the domination the gay agenda seeks to have in the culture. It comes from a major player in the gay community, Masha Gessen, who also happens to be a well-known author. She openly admits, "It's no brainer that [homosexuals] should have the right to marry, but I also think equally that it's a no brainer that the institution of marriage should not exist. ... Fighting for gay marriage generally involves lying about what we are going to do with marriage when we get there—because we lie that the institution of marriage is not going to change, and that is a lie. The institution of marriage is going to change, and it should change. And again, I don't think it should exist. And I don't like taking part in creating fictions about my life."[2]

Talk about being candid. The hardcore leftist gay activists make it abundantly clear that it's not about equality of marriage. It's not even about marrying the person they love. Rather, the truth of the matter is that it's a hostile takeover. It's about the gay agenda—the Gaystapo—doing whatever is necessary to destroy natural marriage. It's time for you and your family to stop ignoring this. We must all realize the threats and the intensified danger many

Christians are experiencing because they won't comply to the demands of the gay agenda.

Memories Pizza (IN)	Gay Mafia	Result
The owner of the restaurant said in an interview that although they serve "gays," she wouldn't cater for a same-sex wedding.	Death threats. Harassing the owners at their restaurant. Threats of suing.	The family had to close down their restaurant. However, thanks to many supporters, the family received almost a million dollars and have since reopened for business.
Masterpiece Cake Shop (CO)	**Gay Mafia**	**Result**
Jack Phillips declined to bake a cake for a same-sex couple's wedding on grounds it would violate his Christian faith.	Used the Colorado Civil Rights Commission to order Mr. Phillips to bake the cake or be severely fined. Diann Rice, State Commissioner, likened Christians to slave owners and Nazis.	Mr. Phillips forced to appeal, costing him a lot of time and money. This was all because he respectfully declined to bake a cake because it went against his faith.
Görtz Haus Gallery (IA)	**Gay Mafia**	**Result**
Richard and Betty Odgaard (devout Mennonites) respectfully declined hosting a gay wedding at their wedding chapel.	Homosexuals targeted and attacked this charming little chapel with the sole purpose to see it shut down.	The Odgaards received vulgar and hate-filled messages. Their business eventually closed down.

Sweet Cakes by Melissa (OR)	Gay Mafia	Result
Melissa and Aaron Klein declined to bake a wedding cake for a lesbian couple because, they said, it went against their Christian faith.	LGBT activists launched a boycott and continued to harass the Kleins and the vendors they did business with.	The Kleins have been dragged into court, with damages in the hundreds of thousands. They closed the doors to their business shortly after the boycott.

Elaine Photography (NM)	Gay Mafia	Result
Jonathan and Elaine Huguenin politely declined photographing a same-sex commitment ceremony.	Even though the lesbian couple found a different photographer for less money, Vanessa Willock filled a complaint with the New Mexico Human Rights Commission.	The Huguenins were taken to court and forced to pay for Willock's legal fees. One justice wrote that the Huguenins "now are compelled by law to compromise the very religious beliefs that inspire their lives," adding "it is the price of citizenship."

How does it make you feel when you read about these assaults on people's religious freedoms? More specifically, how does it make you feel knowing that the Gay Mafia is only after small businesses that are run by Christians? Think about it. We don't see LGBT activists boycotting Muslim-owned businesses, do we?

No doubt it's extremely upsetting. But more than that, we should be motivated by these cases. We should take a stand for our brothers and sisters in the Lord. We should stand strong against these attacks and make our voices heard. We must not allow the Gay Mafia to override our religious rights and enforce their lifestyles on us. It is un-American to impose unjust laws that strong-arm citizens to express and promote ideas that are contrary to their First Amendment rights.

The cases listed above are tragic. Each one of these Americans are just trying to make an honest living. They worked hard to achieve the dream of being a small business owner, to live the American dream, and to provide for their families. And yet they were targeted, they were maligned, and they were hunted down, and dragged through the coals. All because of what? All because they politely (without any abuse or inhumane treatment) declined to provide services to same-sex couples.

We have respect for each one of these Christians, not only because they didn't cave in to the societal norms around them, but because they didn't retaliate and do anything to blow their witness of Christ. They didn't give into the bully tactics of the Gay Mafia. Each one of these Americans stood up for what they believe in. And no jail time or court order fines would intimidate them to reject their religious convictions and cater to a lifestyle they believe to be a sin.

A giant in the Christian faith is Dr. James Dobson. In one of his newsletters, Dr. Dobson expressed his utter regret of the SCOTUS decision to legalize same-sex marriage in the summer of 2015. Dr. Dobson stated, "The effort to force Christians to violate their consciences must be opposed with all vigor, regardless of the consequences—primarily because it is unconstitutional. Christians are being chastised, dismissed, harangued, and sued for daring to practice their deeply held convictions in the public square."[3]

Could you imagine Dr. Dobson reading this newsletter to you? Well, in a private meeting, Dr. Dobson pulled this newsletter out and began reading it to us. Tears filled his eyes as he turned to us and passionately challenged that we keep standing strong for biblical truth, no matter the cost. This moment with Dr. Dobson was surreal yet energizing at the same time. What do you say when a figure like Dr. Dobson gives you a challenge like that?

I'll tell you what we said. We said, "Sir, yes sir!" Unless you're mistaken we aren't the only ones charged with the responsibility to stand up for biblical truth. All Christians who profess the name of Jesus Christ are charged to do so. We are all called to stand up for what is right, and to get back into the business of reinforcing biblical truth in marriage, education, government, politics, media, and dare we say it, in the church once again. To take on the Gaystapo taking over America, we need to remain resolute in not giving into their demands. We need to hang tough.

Outlasting the Gay Revolution

One of the most respected Christian leaders, and a wonderful friend to Stand Strong Ministries, is Dr. Michael Brown. One time, after filling in for Dr. Brown on *The Line of Fire*, we went into his study room after the show. He had a room full of books in German, Greek, and Hebrew. Let's just say we felt very dumb. Dr. Brown is a brilliant scholar, yet a humble servant of God.

For the last decade and a half, Dr. Brown has taken on the gay agenda, and he does it with grace and truth. He has written extensively on the activism of homosexuals and discusses appropriate ways to engage homosexuals that honor Christ. In *Outlasting the Gay Revolution*, Dr. Brown openly spells out eight principles to help Americans with conservative and biblical values stand strong in the midst of homosexual revolution. This is vitally important because same-sex marriage is "the principle threat to freedom of religion, speech, and conscience in America."[4]

Here are the eight principles Dr. Brown gives to help Christians stand strong in the midst of the homosexual revolution:

1. Never compromise your convictions.
2. Take the high moral ground.
3. Sexual purity trumps sexual anarchy.
4. Refuse to redefine marriage.
5. Celebrate gender distinctions.
6. Keep propagating the truth until the lies are dispelled.
7. Factor in the God factor.
8. Be determined to write the last chapter of the book.

Though we can't stress it enough, the truth is that we need more conservative-minded Americans applying these eight principles to their daily lives, not only for exercising the freedoms we all treasure, but to actively fight against the Gay Mafia that seeks to suppress them.

Sadly, many Christians today have either compromised by accepting the belief that homosexuality is not a sin, or have turned away in silence out of fear. But we want you to know that these eight principles have been a tremendous blessing to us, and we believe they will be to you as well. So don't be frightened, and try not to show hatred toward the gay community. Gays need to see Christians living out the eternal gospel (Proverbs 14:25; Colossians 4:5–6). They need to see a willingness to engage in conversation, especially if and when we disagree.

As we seek to live out the eight principles provided by Dr. Brown, we must make sure we don't neglect prayer. Prayer is the key to holding fast during these times. It has the power to unlock the power of heaven. Paul wrote to the Romans, "Be joyful in hope, patient in affliction, *faithful in prayer*" (Romans 12:12). We must persevere through whatever challenges or hardships come our way. But in order to do so, we all must devote our lives to prayer.

Could you imagine what would happen if millions of faithful

prayer warriors prayed against the gay agenda? What would happen if millions of Christians were broken over those enslaved in the homosexual lifestyle? The more we engage with those in the LGBT community, the greater our love and commitment has become in reaching homosexuals with the love and forgiveness of Jesus Christ. But to do so, we all have to be prayed up, willing to meet the need, and to remain standing against the gay agenda with bold conviction.

ISIS: Death to America

Since the formation of ISIS, America has not only underestimated this growing threat but she has failed in putting a plan together to eliminate it. As a matter of fact, James Clapper, director of National Intelligence, flat-out admitted, "We underestimated ISIL [the Islamic State] and overestimated the fighting capability of the Iraqi army. ... I didn't see the collapse of the Iraqi security force in the north coming. I didn't see that. It boils down to predicting the will to fight, which is an imponderable."[5] That statement came from the top dog of intelligence.

As of this writing, there's still no strategic plan for defeating the growing threat of ISIS. One would think by now our military has a plan, but it doesn't. Can you ever think of a time when the greatest military in the world would be so confused and disorganized? If ISIS has proven time and time again that they pose a threat to the survival of America, then what on earth is our administration doing to stop it? How many times does ISIS need to say they are coming to kill Americans in the streets before we take them seriously? How many beheadings do we need to watch before we do something about it? How many cities does ISIS need to pillage? How many more women and children need to be raped before America decides to put an end to these sadistic acts?

He told me that according to Islam he is allowed to rape an unbeliever. He said by raping me he is drawing closer to God.

—A twelve-year-old Yezidi girl

A good friend of mine (Jason), and an expert on militant Islam, is Erick Stakelbeck. Erick is a man of God and a gifted communicator and journalist. He makes his living investigating and reporting on the threats that come out of Islam. In his excellent book, *ISIS Exposed*, Erick writes, "ISIS and its followers are adherents of Jihadist-Salafism, the most extreme and violent interpretation of Islam." He then continues:

To say that ISIS's emergence has captured the attention of Islamists worldwide would be an understatement. The prospect of a reborn Islamic superpower dominating the world stage has loomed large in the imaginations of Muslim radicals for almost a century; ever since the last caliphate came to an end in 1924 after the collapse of the Turkish-led Ottoman Empire, Islamists great and small have pined for its return.[6]

To go deeper on the threat of ISIS, I called Erick to ask him a few direct questions to help us get a better understanding of ISIS. Here's a portion of that conversation.

Jason: Erick, what is the end goal of ISIS?

Erick: No matter what the radical Islamic group is—Hamas, the Muslim Brotherhood, al-Qaeda—what they want is to establish a global caliphate. Now a caliphate is a union of every Muslim nation that is united economically, militarily, and politically. It is ruled by Islamic Sharia law, and Muslims want to impose that upon the world. At this time, ISIS has already declared the caliphate—an Islamic State in Iraq and Syria.

Jason: So how did ISIS become so powerful?

Erick: Well, ISIS has gained so much notoriety because of this revised caliphate that we are seeing take place in the world today. Islamists are rallying behind ISIS because they declared the caliphate in the heart of the Middle East. The Muslim Brotherhood was founded in Egypt in 1928 for similar reasons like ISIS—to establish a worldwide caliphate. However, it's important to mention that ISIS shouldn't exist. Back in 2006 to 2008, American forces decimated al-Qaeda. The troop surge destroyed their operations, and pushed them back. But years later, President Obama withdrew American forces from Iraq, leaving a massive vacuum, which allowed for a resurgence of al-Qaeda forces. That led to a wave of suicide bombers and assassinations of Iraqi political leaders, turning the resurgence of al-Qaeda in Iraq to stretch its tentacles into the civil unrest in Syria. This resurgence has ultimately led to the rise of ISIS.

Jason: Why should Americans care about ISIS?

Erick: It's difficult for Americans to care about ISIS when there is so much prosperity in America. So many are wrapped up in their own lives, taking selfies, and caring more about the Kardashians than they do about what's happening in the Middle East. Meanwhile, ISIS is blazing a path of destruction across the Middle East, and carrying out genocide against Christians. But Americans should care because our national intelligence has confirmed that there is ISIS-related activity going on in all fifty states. There is a network of ISIS supporters and sympathizers that is spreading all across America. Americans can no longer think ISIS is only in the Middle East. ISIS is in the United States. And ISIS is calling on its followers (in the United States) to rise up and participate in jihad. They call these followers city wolves because their purpose is to carry out citywide terror attacks. Just think back to the Boston bomber—that's an example of these type of terror attacks that ISIS is counting on to happen in America. Their ultimate goal is to turn American cities into guerrilla war zones, and that's why Americans should care. ISIS is here in our backyard.

Jason: Why are some Americans joining ISIS?

Erick: ISIS is attracting Americans through a massive social media campaign that is really appealing to younger Americans. Social media is giving ISIS the advantage of getting their propaganda out to millions every second of every day. Another reason Americans are joining ISIS is because they are recent converts to Islam. Many are troubled people with a proclivity toward violence. Also, if you think about our culture today, so many Americans watch brutally violent movies and play video games that chop people's heads off. ISIS, if you think about it, is the product of its times. So it's no wonder that people who are engaged in a violent culture that glorifies violence, torture, and savagery are drawn to the barbarity of ISIS. People who are violent and disturbed are joining ISIS because they are told that not only will they be beheading people, but they will receive religious sanctioning for it, and when they die they will get into heaven.

Jason: Do you believe the United States will soon see terrorist attacks like the one in Paris?

Erick: Absolutely. We've already seen smaller-scale but deadly Islamic terror attacks in Fort Hood, Boston, Chattanooga, New York City, and Oklahoma over the past few years, not to mention a number of foiled attempts on US soil. The truth is that ever since the terrorist attacks that took place in Mumbai in 2008, Western intelligence agencies feared a similar massacre would be replicated by jihadists in a major Western city. The tactics used and targets hit in Paris certainly echo those used in Mumbai, as do the casualty numbers. With radical Islamists gaining a firm foothold the past few decades in major cities throughout Western Europe, we can, unfortunately, expect more large-scale attacks like we witnessed in Paris, particularly with battle-hardened ISIS "returnees" trickling back into their countries of origin.

You will see when US military and government personnel start getting beheaded in their own homes.

—*ISIS member*

The Seven Phases of Islam

We can no longer afford to ignore the things Erick and others are saying about Islam and ISIS. The threat level is getting higher, and we must respond. This may freak you out, but we feel that you need to know this: there happens to be a book that has this whole Islamic takeover charted out. That's right—there exists a book that lays out each phase for an eventual world domination of Islam. And get this—the goal is to achieve it within twenty years.

In his book *Al-Zarqawi: The Second Generation of Al Qaeda*, Fouad Hussein charts seven phases needed in order for Muslims to achieve final victory, giving the time frame in which to complete each phase. The seven phases are listed below:

- Phase 1: The Muslim Awakening (2000–2003)
- Phase 2: Opening Eyes (2003–2006)
- Phase 3: Arising and Standing Up (2007–2010)
- Phase 4: Collapse (2010–2013)

- Phase 5: Caliphate (2013–2016)
- Phase 6: Total Confrontation (2016–2019)
- Phase 7: Definitive Victory (2020)

Did you catch the final two phases and the dates listed? That's where we are right now at this time in history. As you read this, we are seeing a total confrontation from radical Muslims. What this means is that we will see attacks coming from every side. There will be no more hiding and taking the high road, no more victimization on the part of Muslims. Phase six is an all-out attack against the world.

And remember that in order for Islam to take over the world, they need to downgrade America. We are seeing how easily that can happen. Look what 9/11 did? Then just think of what would happen if mass terrorism breaks out in malls? Schools? Football games? Airports? A few strategic terrorist attacks would have catastrophic results. The death tolls would be in the tens of thousands.

The First of the Storm

On the evening of November 13, 2015, three teams of Islamic State terrorists carried out a deadly string of suicide bombings and shootings on six different sites in France. Explosives were detonated outside the Stade de France stadium, the Bataclan concert hall, and several crowded bars and restaurants. The death toll was 130 people—men, women, and children. Nearly 352 people were injured during the attacks, and almost a hundred of them were in critical condition.

These terrorist attacks were engineered using assault rifles and suicide vests. Within hours of the massacre in Paris, the Islamic State claimed responsibility, calling them "the first of the storm." These catastrophic attacks in France were highly coordinated, and, dreadfully, will not be the last that we see. The scary thing about these attacks is that the terrorists targeted a sports arena, a concert, and local places where people shop and eat. These attacks were a statement to the world that ISIS will attack you when you least expect it. They will target you where you are most vulnerable.

Just a few short weeks after the Paris attacks, the community of San Bernardino, California, was rocked by yet another terrorist attack. A mass shooting by a radicalized Islamic terrorist couple, Syed Farook and his wife, Tashfeen Malik. This terrorist couple went to the Inland Regional Center and opened fire on a crowd of employees at a Christmas party, killing fourteen, and injuring twenty-one more. The massacre had all the signs of terrorism. However, the White House and the mainstream media were too afraid to state the obvious, and they immediately called it work-place violence. But it didn't take long for the FBI to come out stating that they were treating the massacre as an act of terrorism.

Just weeks before the mass killing in San Bernardino, ISIS had issued a decree to all loyal supporters to launch terror attacks in America. The massacre in San Bernardino was such a response. We are no longer living in a time when these kinds of terrorist attacks are seen on the movie screen. They are happening in real life, and they are happening more frequently.

Since 9/11, there have been hundreds of terrorist attacks around the world, many of which have been stopped thanks to the intelligence and cooperation of different agencies. But when you think back to some of the deadliest attacks, it's both sad and frightening. On March 11, 2004, in Madrid, Spain, during morning rush hour, bombs were detonated on four commuter trains, killing 191 people and injuring more than 1,800 more. On September 1–3, 2004, in Beslan, Russia, Islamist gunmen took over a school with over 1,000 hostages, most of them children. After the siege ended, the final death toll was over 330, and more than 800 were injured. On November 26–29, 2008, in Mumbai, India, there were multiple coordinated attacks by ten gunmen in India's largest city, where 172 people where killed. And on October 31, 2015, in Egypt, a Russian A321 airliner was blown up by a homemade bomb, killing all 224 people on board the plane. This is what Americans can no longer ignore.

ISIS is on the move. They are spreading and will not stop until they accomplish their mission. That mission is to inflict as much massive casualty and panic around the globe as they possibly can. Massive terrorism all over the country will send us into a national panic. The 9/11 terrorist attack singlehandedly revolutionized our national security. We have spent untold billions of dollars fighting global terrorism, and trying to beef up security at airports, sporting events, and everywhere else that attracts people. Terrorism not only has taken the lives of countless civilians, but it has also run our military and economy to the ground.

America must have an aggressive plan to fight ISIS. We can no longer afford dodging the term "Islamic radicals" in order to be politically correct. We must know our enemy if we plan to defeat that enemy.

Militant Secularism

In Winter Haven, Florida, a professor at Polk State College by the name of Lance Russum is flunking students who don't agree with his atheism. To get a feel for what Professor Russum thinks of Christianity, his cover photo on Facebook was of a picture of Jesus Christ giving the middle finger (until he took it down). Think about how offensive that is, not to mention how unprofessional. Parents pay big money for their kids to get a good education, and is this the kind of offensive behavior they are getting from their professors? Yeah. Pretty much.

For the most part, Christians and atheists get along. No doubt they have their fair share of debates, arguments, and disagreements, but despite the ongoing feuds, much of the two sides remain civil. But today, a militant secularism is on the rise and its very existence is to remove any trace of religion from society. So it's important to understand the difference between a secularist and a militant secularist.

The average secularist has his or her doubts about God and religion, and may get involved in a few debates over the separation of church and state. Militant secularists, on the other hand, seek to personally attack and abuse any religious person who voices their religious beliefs and/or disagrees with secularism. Simply put, militant secularists are bullies. They don't seek to have reasonable conversations, and they certainly don't treat people of faith with any respect.

In the mind of a militant secularist, they are doing a service to humankind by actively eradicating doctrines of religion in place of their own. And they don't consider it infringing upon a person's First Amendment rights either. The way they see it is that they are stopping dangerous propaganda from harming people. Here are a few comments from some militant atheists:

> Explain to me how a book that's written by God who's perfect has so much—it's pro-slavery, pro-polygamy, it's homophobic. Yeah, God in the Old Testament is a psychotic mass murderer. You know, this, I mean, there's so many things in it. And I always say to my religious friends, you know, if a pool had even one turd in it, would you jump in?
>
> —BILL MAHER, HBO's *Real Time*

> Organized religion, wielding power over the community, is antithetical to the process of what modern democracy should define as liberty. The sooner we are without it, the better.
>
> —LAWRENCE KRAUSS, American theoretical physicist

> Jesus, the Easter bunny and other delusions: Just say no!
>
> —PETER BOGHOSSIAN, philosophy professor

Let's get back to Professor Russum for a moment. It seems this guy loves picking on young Christians. In one of his classes, Russum required students to keep a journal that he would read and review. After reading one of his student's journal that stated, "I believe in God," he responded, "You need to drop my class." Why does the student need to drop his class? All the student affirmed was his personal belief in God, which is a right every American has. But not according to Russum.

Bully Alert

Truth is, professors like Russum are allowed (and even encouraged) to attack religious students in class every day, while Christian conservative professors are being accused of discriminatory practices in the classroom, hunted down, publically defamed, and eventually fired by the university.

Take, for instance, Professor Carol Swain at the prestigious Vanderbilt University, in Nashville, Tennessee. A petition was sent around campus for students to sign, supporting the firing of Professor Swain. The reason for the firing? She is a black female who is conservative … and, oh, she just happens to be Christian too. BINGO! That's it.

Professor Swain represents everything the progressives ruling the universities hate. And so, these liberal students and faculty members came out hard on Professor Swain, making derogatory claims about her professorship and personal demeanor. Just take a look at what a portion of the petition against Professor Swain claims:

> Over the past few years, Professor Carol Swain has become synonymous with bigotry, intolerance, and unprofessionalism. While Swain first and foremost has a right to her personal beliefs and the right to freedom of speech within

and outside of the classroom, it recently came to the attention of the Vanderbilt community that Carol Swain has let her hate-filled prejudices negatively impact her work, our student body, and Vanderbilt's reputation.[7]

But here's the problem: none of these allegations are true. Professor Swain has never insulted, abused, ridiculed, or discriminated any of her Vanderbilt students. As a matter of fact, the source of these accusations came from students outside Professor Swain's classroom. There's not a shred of evidence proving Swain has ever demonstrated unprofessional behavior in class or has ever portrayed a "hate-filled prejudice" toward students.

According to those who best know Professor Swain, the very opposite is true. She is very professional, she is extremely smart, and she has gone above and beyond to make her students feel accepted and loved. And yet the chancellor of the university, before any proof of these accusations were found true, supported the petition against Professor Swain. This is nothing more than a double standard.

If you are a liberal atheist who hates organized religion, then you qualify to teach at the university level. But if you support natural marriage, are pro-life, read your Bible, attend church, and vote conservative—well, then you have no future as an academic professor at any leading university.

Atheistic Evangelism

Peter Boghossian, whom we quoted above, recently wrote a book entitled *A Manual for Creating Atheists*. Dr. Boghossian doesn't hold back when explaining his reasoning behind the book. In an interview about his book, he had this to say:

> The New Atheists paved the way. They started the movement. This book picks up and gives people specific tools. It is a road

map. It is a tool book. It is a guide. It is a manual to help move the conversation forward and actually do something. It is a call to humanists and atheists and skeptics and philosophers. It is a specific road map that they can use to make a difference every day. Anyone and everyone. People who have religious relatives, people who have religious friends, or faithful friends. People who engage with others of faith at any time. I would like to create at least ten thousand people—a minimum of ten thousand people. I look at faith as a virus. We give many inoculations to people—five, ten, fifteen people—on a daily basis. No matter whether it is a woman at the bank who wears a cross every time I see her, I go out of my way to wait in her line and then I immediately begin the intervention. Everyone, I'm looking for ten thousand people to start off with. Ten thousand people armed with these tools that can go into the streets and into the PTA, everywhere the faithful reside, into their own homes, and families and talk people out of their faith, out of their superstitions, and into reason and rationality. I think ten thousand people is a very achievable number.[8]

This militancy is a form of atheistic evangelism. Atheists like Dr. Boghossian are literally in full-time "ministry" attacking Christianity and converting Christians to atheism by getting them to deny Jesus Christ as Lord and Savior. This is a cultural war—a war raging over the hearts and minds of our young people.

This atheistic evangelism has sparked a flame in our culture. The anti-Christian Freedom from Religion Foundation (FFRF), which is an organization purposed to oust Christianity in America, is a demonstration of this growing hostility. On their website they state that their mission is "to promote the constitutional principle of separation of state and church, and to educate the public on matters relating to nontheism." The mission of FFRF sounds innocuous, but it's their interpretation of "separation of church and state" and education on "nontheistic" views that are dangerous.

In the past few years, the FFRF has played a vital role in removing Ten Commandment monuments, "In God We Trust" off of our currency, chaplains from college sports and from the military, and the Pledge of Allegiance from schools and they have successfully banned the National Day of Prayer from public schools all across the country. One of their big pushes is to get every single Bible out of hotels. The FFRF call the Holy Bible in hotels an "unwelcome religious propaganda in the bedside table."

You don't have to go back too far in history to recount what kind of persecution and destruction militant atheism brings to the world. From 1917 to 1989, in the USSR, millions of Christians were killed because of their faith. Christians were seen as a barrier to the Soviet Union. They weren't allowed to give to the poor, attend church, and give out religious literature. Anything religious was deemed illegal and was so banned by the Soviet Union. Churches were confiscated, clergy were arrested, beaten, and many of them killed. Students were indoctrinated in Soviet propaganda, and anyone or anything that opposed atheistic teachings were considered an enemy of the state.

This is the path America is following. If Christians don't stand up and reinforce biblical truth in the culture, then organizations like the FFRF will have the last word. They will take what was once a theistic society—one built on a Judeo-Christian ethic—and turn it into an atheistic society that is based on godless ideas that eradicate religious people.

America's Divorce with Israel

To say US-Israeli relations are rocky is an understatement. No question these are turbulent times for the United States and Israel. The liberal policies of the Obama Administration have led to strained relations and mounting problems among the two democratic allies. What was once considered a good marriage between the two nations has now resulted in a separation (with no reconciliation in sight). And if the tension between the United States and Israel continues, then divorce between these two nations is inevitable.

How did this happen? How did we get here? America has always had Israel's back, but now Obama and many US officials have caused considerable damage to the relationship with Israel. Why? You don't separate from someone you care about, and you certainly don't leave them in harm's way. But tragically, that's what America is doing. We have abandoned Israel.

Israel is surrounded by al-Qaeda, Hamas, Hezbollah, and ISIS. All of these encircle Israel with the intent to wipe her off the map. And as if that's not enough, these same terrorist groups want the same fate for America as well. So rather than keep defending God's sacred people, we have chosen to discard our allegiance to God and Israel and exchange them for swift judgment. But this wasn't always the case.

Since Israel became a sovereign state on May 14, 1948, America has supported Israel's right to exist, and has made much of its foreign policy around peace in the Middle East. The Israelis have respectfully looked to the United States for political, financial, and military assistance for decades. The two countries have shared an important relationship unlike any other relationship in the world. In return, America has not only viewed Israel as an important ally in that region, but as a strong democratic model of freedom, religion, and perseverance.

> Israel was not created in order to disappear—Israel will endure and flourish. It is the child of hope and home of the brave. It can neither be broken by adversity nor demoralized by success. It carries the shield of democracy and it honors the sword of freedom.[9]
> —*John F. Kennedy*

Just thinking about the survival of the Jews in the midst of historical persecution is truly remarkable. President Ronald Reagan proudly proclaimed, "In Israel, free men and women are every day demonstrating the power of courage and faith. Back in 1948 when Israel was founded, pundits claimed the new country could never survive. Today, no one questions that Israel is a land of stability and democracy in a region of tyranny and unrest. ... America has never flinched from its commitment to the State of Israel—a commitment which remains unshakable."[10] But this appreciation for Israel goes further back than when Israel became a nation in 1948. The great Thomas Jefferson said this about Israel: "I will insist that the Hebrews have done more to civilize man than any other nation."[11]

Our two nations have a lot in common, when you think about it. We were both founded by immigrants escaping religious persecution in other lands. We both have built vibrant democracies. Both our countries are founded on certain basic beliefs, that there is an Almighty God who watches over the affairs of men and values every life. These ties have made us natural allies, and these ties will never be broken.[12]

—*George W. Bush*

So when Obama took office and started to impose his radical views about Israel on the American people, it caused an uproar. And that is not a political statement; it's a fact. Obama came into office promoting a pro-Palestinian policy, not a pro-Israeli one. Despite the threat posed by Iran, Obama nevertheless advanced a nuclear accord with them. Netanyahu referred to the Iranian nuclear deal as "a grave danger" to Israel's survival. It's unbelievable to think that America has not only jeopardized its relations with God's chosen people, but our national leaders have deliberately put Israel and the American people in harm's way by advancing a nuclear deal with Iran.

Iran is considered the most dangerous and most radically Islamic country in the world. This is the same place where the Iranian supreme leader, the Ayatollah Ali Khamenei, said that the "mission of the Islamic Republic of Iran is to erase Israel from the map of the region." These are the same people who refer to the United States of America as the "Great Satan," and have been seen burning the American flag and chanting, "Death to America."

Iran is the number one state sponsor of terror, a nation known to harbor, promote, train, and send out Islamic terrorists all over the globe. And yet the United States has decided that it's in our best interests to work with Iran? The Iran that poses a serious threat to our national security?

Lest we forget, Iran has made it perfectly clear what they will do if they get their hands on nuclear weapons. They will use them to blow up Israel, America, and the West. In their minds, a nuclear attack on the world isn't a bad thing; rather, it's a good thing. A nuclear holocaust is necessary to usher in the Muslim Savior, Mahdi, and bring global security under Shi'ite domination.

So for America to be strategically investing itself in helping Iran doesn't make any sense whatsoever, but it does when you consider how godless America has become. Turning our back on Israel and working with Iran never happened when America aligned herself more closely to God and prayer, and was more heavily influenced by Christians who care for the safety of Israel. Thus, the departure from Israel and the alliances with Islamic states bear testimony to how troubled and lost we've become as a nation.

The Time Is Now

In the midst of the threats addressed above (in chapters 6 and 7), there is an even greater danger that has been building up for quite some time. It's a movement that is gaining momentum and that believes the Constitution, our founding document, is restrictive, archaic, and just plain old. Essentially, this view thinks the Constitution needs a face-lift. It needs to be altered and changed for the times in which we live today. It suggests that the framers where nothing but old white religious nut jobs who dreamed of a utopia whereby black people were slaves and their religion ruled the towns. Now anything that runs contrary to the mainstream ideology is deemed intolerant and bad for society. Like, let's see here—Christianity?

To see how this view is taking shape and having an effect on society today, just pay attention to the growing cases of Christians being prosecuted for their faith. Christians, and this is no joke, are being hunted down by the government because it's believed they are a threat to American progress. Teachers are being fired for sharing their faith in class. Coaches are losing their jobs because they prayed with their teams. Chaplains are being released from the military because they believe Jesus Christ is the only way to heaven. Hunting Christians is in season right now. But if we fail to act, it will become a year-round sport. We certainly don't want to see the day if and when this happens. But there's one thing for sure—we aren't going to sit around hoping it doesn't. All the signs point to a coming persecution that most Christians living in America have absolutely no clue is coming.

That's why we are sounding the alarm. We need to be in the business of informing, protecting, and mobilizing Christians to take a stand—to stand for what they believe in, and to do what's necessary to share it with those who adamantly disagree.

When the stakes were high, General Washington led his American troops into battle. Washington and his men knew what they were fighting for. Their fight wasn't against the redcoats; they were fighting for the future freedoms of all Americans. And so on July 2, 1776, Washington boldly declared to his troops:

The time is now near at hand which must probably determine whether Americans are to be freemen or slaves; whether they are to have any property they can call their own; whether their houses and farms are to be pillaged and destroyed, and themselves consigned to a state of wretchedness from which no human efforts will deliver them.[13]

He then continued, "The fate of unborn millions will now depend, under God, on the courage and conduct of this army. Our cruel and unrelenting enemy leaves us no choice but a brave resistance, or the most abject submission. We have, therefore, to resolve to conquer or die."[14]

The time is now. The enemy back then were the redcoats, and although things have drastically changed today, in many ways the fight is the same. Washington wasn't just fighting a military; he was fighting against an ideology that believed Americans had no right to be free from tyranny.

The same fight remains for us today. We are fighting against an ideology that is trying to overtake our country. This ideology seeks to strip each American of his or her rights, and make everyone a slave to the demands of this oppressive movement. But like Washington and his brave troops, we too need to rise up against any and all ideologies that threaten our sacred faith. We, the church, need to resolve to conquer any ideology that opposes the Christian faith, or at least die trying.

STAND STRONG: COURAGE

Courageous people are hard to find, especially in the times we live in. Most Americans are living in fear and are overcome by the growing threats that are overtaking America. And so to live courageously we must first learn to face our fears and have faith in God that He will give us the strength to overcome them. So we must ask ourselves, what fears am I facing right now that are preventing me from living a life of courage? Secondly, why am I allowing fear to rule my life, and not faith?

We need to decide what kind of life we want to live. Do we want to live a natural life of fear, or do we want to live a supernatural life of faith and courage? Instead of giving excuses as to why we are overcome by fear, we should rather start declaring all the reasons in faith why we are living out a courageous life for the good of others.

CHAPTER 8

A NOBLE VINE:
THEN AND NOW

Cursed be all learning that is contrary
to the cross of Christ.[1]
—JONATHAN DICKSON, FIRST PRESIDENT
OF PRINCETON UNIVERSITY

Amerias's creation was unique in the history of the world. Government led by the people, of the people, and for the people stood in sharp contrast to the European nations of the time. Why did America choose a new attempt at "a more perfect union" then? The answer can be found in both their experiences and their faith. The early American settlers were deeply religious people who often came to this new land for the opportunity to worship and instruct their children according to the teachings of God's Word.

Jonathan Edwards, often known as America's greatest theologian, served as the president of Princeton in the eighteenth century. In speaking of the desire of America's early inhabitants to develop a godly nation, he wrote, "When England grew corrupt, God brought over a number of pious persons and planted them in New England, and *this land was planted with a noble vine.*"[2]

Thanksgiving: America Began with Gratitude to God

A look at the earliest Europeans to inhabit our nation reflects the words of Edwards. For example, a tombstone inscription of John Cooke found in Fairhaven, Massachusetts, offers a memorial to those who traveled on the *Mayflower* to America. It reads:

> Sacred to the memory of John Cooke
> Who was buried here in 1695
> The last surviving male Pilgrim
> Of those who came over in the Mayflower
> The first white settler of this town
> And the pioneer in its religious
> Moral and business life
> A man of character and integrity
> And the trusted agent for this
> part of the Commonwealth
> Of the Old Colonial
> Civil Government of Plymouth.

Regarding the *Mayflower* Pilgrims and what we now celebrate as Thanksgiving, America's founders recognized that the gifts of personal salvation and national blessing were from the hand of God. Truly, America's miraculous birth and subsequent prosperity has been equaled by no other nation. From the founding period until the present day, God has graciously protected and provided for America. Our ancestors clearly knew that God was responsible for America's liberty and security, and they thanked God accordingly.

In light of these facts, it is distressing to read modern textbook accounts that misrepresent the origin of the Thanksgiving holiday. Some schools and colleges today simply ignore the role that Christianity played in America's history, and the subject of Thanksgiving is often minimized or distorted. Many persons have been conditioned to believe that the Pilgrims instituted the Thanksgiving celebration to show gratitude to Native Americans for their help upon arriving. In order to fully understand and appreciate what Thanksgiving was truly about, however, let's look back at some historical facts.

Organized Thanksgiving services were held in Virginia as early as 1607, but the first Thanksgiving Festival was held in 1621. The Pilgrims had left Plymouth, England, on September 6, 1620. The *Mayflower's* 102 passengers were at sea for over two months, arriving in Massachusetts in late November. On December 11, 1620, the passengers signed the Mayflower Compact, America's first document of civil government, which heavily influenced all subsequent founding documents. It stated that the Pilgrims' purpose was "the Glory of God, and the advancement of the Christian faith."

Once on land, shelters and rough living quarters were quickly built. Yet by the spring, one-half of the Pilgrims had died. The summer's farming efforts yielded a bountiful crop, and local Native Americans assisted this good harvest. On December 13, 1621, the Pilgrims began a three-day feast to thank God and celebrate with the native people of the land. They were fervent in their prayers and thanked God for their survival. The words of Pilgrim Edward Winslow give insight into the meaning of the event:

> Our harvest being gotten in, our Governor sent four men on fowling, so that we might, after a special manner, rejoice together. … Many of the Indians came amongst us, and their greatest King, Massossoit, with some 90 men, whom for three days we entertained and feasted. … And although it be not always so plentiful as it was at this time with us, yet by the goodness of God, we are far from want.[3]

God's gracious provision prompted many leaders to call for days of thanksgiving. Two years after the first Thanksgiving celebration,

Governor William Bradford proclaimed November 29, 1623, to be an official day of thanks. He wrote of the praise that was owed to God, for both harvest and freedom. Bradford decreed: "I do proclaim that all ye Pilgrims, with your wives and little ones, do gather at ye meeting house, there to listen to ye pastor and render thanksgiving to ye Almighty God for His blessings."[4]

Other national days of thanksgiving to God were declared and passed into law as the years went by. Educators of our day depict Thomas Jefferson as a thoroughly secular man, but as the governor of Virginia, Jefferson proclaimed November 11, 1777, as a day of "Public and solemn Thanksgiving to Almighty God."

Several other states passed Thanksgiving decrees that carried similar sentiments. In 1789, with the unanimous approval of Congress, George Washington proclaimed that a National Day of Thanksgiving be observed on Thursday, November 26, of that same year. In his official proclamation, Washington wrote that America was to thank God for His many blessings, and ask God's forgiveness for national and personal sins.

Blessings Taken for Granted

It is clear that our forefathers were a thankful people, and the object of their worship was God. In our times, Americans seem to take for granted the blessings of freedom, liberty, security, and plenty. We enjoy the best, and we enjoy it in abundance. Perhaps you have gone through this day without giving much thought to what was involved to make it possible for you to enjoy in the first place. We would all do well to reflect on these words by America's sixth president, John Quincy Adams, who wrote, "Posterity—you will never know how much it has cost my generation to preserve your freedom. I hope you will make good use of it."[5]

It is time that we all take a fresh look at how good God has been to us. The older I (Alex) become, the more patriotic I become as well. Let us be reminded of what a privilege it is to live in the United States of America. And may we gain a deeper awareness of the responsibilities that come with such great blessings.

The Founding of America's Educational Institutions

From its earliest years, part of forming a more perfect union included the development of educational institutions in America. What did the founders and educational leaders of earlier America believe should be taught? Thomas Jefferson authored the educational plan for the Washington, DC, school system. The first two books he installed as reading materials were the Watts Hymnal and the Holy Bible. He justified his book choices by writing, "The Bible is the cornerstone of American liberty. A student's perusal of this sacred volume will make them a better citizen."[6]

Jefferson was not alone in this viewpoint either. Congress passed the Northwest Ordinance in 1789, requiring that religion, morality, and knowledge be taught in schools and other means of education, as a prerequisite for statehood in the United States. In 1791, Benjamin Rush published a pamphlet entitled "A Defence [sic] of the Use of the Bible in Schools." Though the entire pamphlet is fascinating, what we found most interesting was the assumptions upon which it was built. These five propositions were apparently commonly held among those in his time. He wrote:

> It is now several months since I promised to give you my reasons for preferring the Bible as a schoolbook to all other compositions. Before I state my arguments, I shall assume the five following propositions:
>
> 1. That Christianity is the only true and perfect religion; and that in proportion as mankind adopt its principles and obey its precepts they will be wise and happy.
> 2. That a better knowledge of this religion is to be acquired by reading the Bible than in any other way.

3. That the Bible contains more knowledge necessary to man in his present state than any other book in the world.
4. That knowledge is most durable, and religious instruction most useful, when imparted in early life.
5. That the Bible, when not read in schools, is seldom read in any subsequent period of life.[7]

As a result, early education focused heavily upon Christian themes. Colonial children learned the alphabet from the *New England Primer*. The second edition, which was published in 1691, was used by thousands of students. It used Bible verses and Christian rhymes to teach the alphabet. Children learned both reading and Christian principles at the same time. For example, the alphabet—A through Z—contained a panorama of biblical allusions:

A: In Adam's fall we sinned all.
B: Heaven to find, the Bible mind.
C: Christ crucified, for sinners died.

Also in the back of this school textbook is what is entitled "A short Prayer to be used every Morning." It stated:

O Lord, our heavenly Father, almighty and everlasting God. I most humbly thank thee for thy great mercy and goodness in preserving and keeping me from all perils and dangers of this night past, and bringing me safely in the beginning of this day; defend me, O Lord, in the same, with thy mighty power; and grant, that this day I may fall into no sin, neither run into danger, but that all my doings may be ordered by thy governance, to do always that which is righteous in thy sight, through Jesus Christ our Lord. Amen.[8]

Yet in the 1960s public prayer was removed from America's schools. Today, organizations routinely threaten legal action against the smallest inclusions of Christian themes in public schools. In some New York public schools, Muslim holidays are celebrated, while Christian holidays such as Christmas, Good Friday, or Easter are neglected. Our nation's founders would find such practices strange if not outright un-American.

America's Early Colleges

America's first universities were founded to teach the Bible and to prepare servants for Christian ministry. Of the first 108 universities founded in America, 106 were distinctly Christian, including the first, Harvard University, which was chartered in 1636. The original Harvard Student Handbook had, as its first rule, that all students applying must know both Latin and Greek, in order that they may understand the Scriptures:

> Let every student be plainly instructed and earnestly pressed to consider well, the main end of his life and studies, is, to know God and Jesus Christ, which is eternal life, John 17:3; and therefore to lay Jesus Christ as the only foundation for our children to follow the moral principles of the Ten Commandments.

Harvard was founded in 1636. In 1796, they printed an update of their constitution, which stated, "If you doubt the inspiration of the Scriptures, you are subject to the immediate dismissal from Harvard." These words bear a stark contrast with the beliefs found on college campuses today.

Princeton College was founded in 1746. Its first president was Reverend Jonathan Dickson. The philosophy of education that Reverend Dickson brought to the leadership of Princeton College included, "Cursed be all learning that is contrary to the Cross of Christ." This was Princeton's founding statement. In addition, every president of Princeton was a minister until 1902. After Reverend Dickson, Reverend John Witherspoon served as president.

As we will recall, Witherspoon was a signer of the Declaration, a member of Continental Congress, served on over a hundred congressional committees, and was an ordained clergyman.

Yale University's founding statement was, "God is the giver of all wisdom." William Lyon Phelps, an early president of Yale University, wrote, "I thoroughly believe in a university education for both men and women; but I believe knowledge of the Bible without a college course is more valuable than a college course without the Bible."[9]

America's earliest educational institutions were so tied to a Christian-based curriculum that when a Philadelphia school announced in 1844 that it would teach morality but not religion, and thus exclude Christianity from its classroom discussions, the case was taken to the US Supreme Court. Regarding the question of whether schools could or should teach Christianity or not, the 1844 court ruled:

> Why may not the Bible, and especially the New Testament be read and taught as divine revelation in the (school)—its general precepts expounded, and its glorious principles of morality inculcated? Where can the purest principles of morality be learned so clearly or so perfectly as from the New Testament?[10]

How Can We Form a "More Perfect Union" Today?

No one would disagree that much has changed since early American times. In contrast, some argue that there are as many views of government as there are people. In other words, people have their own unique view of what government is and how it should function. However, Dr. Wayne Grudem suggests that Christians tend to look at government in one of six ways, the first five of which are based on mistaken interpretations of Scripture.[11] What faulty assumption do we often make? Which view is the best biblical approach for forming a more perfect union? Let's take a look at each view and determine how we can help America stand strong.

View 1: Compel Religion

This view of religion includes the idea of *requiring* individuals to follow a particular religion. From the time of Christianity becoming the official religion of the Roman Empire in the fourth century until the founding of America in 1776, this view was the norm in many parts of Europe. Rather than allowing personal freedom of religion, the government adopted one religion that became the standard for all its citizens. In this case, the Roman Catholic Church existed as the official state religion. In England, the Church of England served as the national church. The corruption that often took place in these systems influenced the creation of the United States as a land that allowed religious freedom.

View 2: Exclude Religion

A second view sometimes taken regarding Christianity and government is to exclude religion from government matters. Rather than deal with a state religion or competing views of religion, this view seeks "freedom from religion," resulting in secularism. This view grew in popularity in the twentieth century in the United States as daily prayers were removed from public schools and political correctness sought to remove religious influences from national monuments and documents. Yet there is no government that truly excludes religion, nor can it. Religion includes issues of worldview, something that influences one's views of law and morality.

View 3: All Government Is Demonic

While all would agree government is far from perfect, some have taken the extreme view that all government is demonic or downright evil. Therefore, Christians should not only stay out of politics, but they should flee from them altogether. However, strong evidence against this view can be found from one of Jesus's closest followers, the apostle Peter.

In 1 Peter 2:13–14, he wrote, "Submit yourselves for the Lord's sake to every human authority: whether to the emperor, as the supreme authority, or to governors, who are sent by him to punish those who do wrong and to commend those who do right." Rather than reject all government as demonic, we are called to submit to governing authorities and to do what is right. We can't do that if we flee from government based on faulty fears that Satan is controlling it.

View 4: Do Evangelism, Not Politics

Another view held by many Christians regarding the role of government is one Grudem labels "do evangelism, not politics." This would include those who teach that Christians should only communicate the gospel message with no involvement in politics whatsoever. At a popular level, many Christians practice this view. They attend church, read the Bible, and pray, yet they do not vote or even know the candidates running for political office in their community or state. Is this what God intended for us as Christians to engage the culture in which we live?

Those who hold this view typically focus on the final earthly command of Jesus known as the Great Commission. In Matthew 28:19–20, He taught, "Therefore go and make disciples of all nations, baptizing them in the name of the Father and of the Son and of the Holy Spirit, and teaching them to obey everything I have commanded you. And surely I am with you always, to the very end of the age." The clear command is to both evangelize and includes "teaching them to obey everything I have commanded you." Certainly this would include the teachings given by the apostles and their associates in the New Testament to pray for governing authorities (1 Timothy 2:1–4), to submit to governing leaders (Romans 13), and to live as salt and light among the unbelieving world (Matthew 5:13–16). Evangelism and politics are both noble endeavors for the followers of Jesus.

View 5: Do Politics, Not Evangelism

While evangelism apart from politics neglects the important biblical call to influence society, there are also believers who seek political change without emphasizing the importance of salvation. Grudem labels this view "do politics, not evangelism." This view may not be openly held by many Christians today, yet there is an inherent danger that in seeking to change laws, believers can sometimes forget the essential spiritual message God has called us to communicate.

You have enemies? Good. That means you've stood up for something, sometime in your life.[12]

—*Winston Churchill*

View 6: Significant Christian Influence on Government

Grudem's sixth category, the one he argues as the correct biblical understanding of Christian involvement in politics, is "significant Christian influence on government." Many biblical examples can be shared to support this view. For example, Daniel once challenged his governing leader, King Nebuchadnezzar, boldly proclaiming, "Therefore, Your Majesty, be pleased to accept my advice: Renounce your sins by doing what is right, and your wickedness by being kind to the oppressed. It may be that then your prosperity will continue" (Daniel 4:27). Rather than stand aside and allow the king's immorality to continue without warning, this biblical prophet stood against sin while being known as a person of integrity who served his government with excellence.

Scripture provides many other examples as well: Joseph is seen as influencing the entire land of Egypt by God's will (Genesis 41–45); Moses calls Pharaoh to exhibit justice and free the Jewish people (Exodus 8:1); Nehemiah serves the king, yet he also serves as part of a spiritual awakening in Israel (Nehemiah 1); Mordecai is put second in command of Persia and foiled an assassination attempt on the king, yet he is faithful to God and helped to rescue the Jewish people (Esther 3; 8–10); Esther served as queen, yet she also fasted for three days and begged the king to save the Jewish people (Esther 4:15–16). Likewise, John the Baptist spoke against the sins of the region's leader while also baptizing in the Jordan River and calling people to repentance (Luke 3:18–20), while Paul shared the gospel with governor Felix (Acts 24:24–25), along with other political leaders, all while serving as a missionary to the non-Jewish (Gentile) world (Romans 1:16–17).

I know not a better rule of reading the Scripture, than to read it through from beginning to end and when we have finished it once, to begin it again.[13]

—*John Newton*

Those who desire to both share the gospel and influence government through living out their biblical beliefs find a rich legacy of God followers in the pages of Scripture. The Bible's tradition includes both an emphasis on personal salvation and holy living found only in Jesus Christ (John 14:6; Acts 4:12), along with numerous examples of believers standing up for godly principles within the political realm in order to influence the society in which they live.

CHAPTER 9

A MORE PERFECT UNION

Those people who will not be governed
by God will be ruled by tyrants.[1]
—WILLIAM PENN

S elf-governance is a noble concept that no political system had ever achieved—at least not until the Constitution of the United States of America. Or shall we say that it was the greatest gift for governance ever bestowed upon a nation of people? Our founders did an incredible thing—they established a government controlled and monitored by the people and for the people.

This is what is meant by self-governance: a governmental system built on the God-given truths that all men are created equal, and thus have the right to govern themselves as a sovereign people, a people who possess basic human rights of life, liberty, and the pursuit of happiness. In modern English, the Preamble of the Constitution reads,

> We the people of the United States, have created and agreed to this Constitution for the United States of America. We have done this in order to make our Union stronger, set standards for justice, keep the peace at home, provide for our

common defense, promote our general well-being, and make sure that the blessings of liberty continue for ourselves and our descendants.[2]

Such rights, according to the Constitution, transcend human government. It's not the government who grants the peoples' rights; rather, it's the government's duty to protect the rights of the people.

Think of it like this: God is the *source* of human rights, and the government is the *security* of those rights. Therefore, according to the founders of our nation, every person is equal before God, equal under the law, and equal in their rights to live as they so choose. But there's one big problem with self-governance: if the self-governed stop believing their right, duty, and responsibility is to protect, live, and preserve freedoms, then self-government ceases to exist.

If angels were to govern men, neither external nor internal controls on government would be necessary. ... [But lacking these] you must first enable the government to control the governed; and in the next place oblige it to control itself.[3]

—*James Madison*

When people neglect to self-govern, naturally a tyrannical government arises in its place. *We the People* becomes *We the Government*, which is exactly what's happening in America right now. Our *more perfect union* is shaping into a *more corrupt faction*, where the interests of the people (along with their individual protected rights) become obsolete.

Disconnected Americans

At this point, the progressive ideology has convinced much of America to exchange the written truths of our more perfect union for a socialist one. Our free markets are not free anymore; they are more like manipulated markets. Federal regulations are at an all-time high. Every day is just another day of forcing regulations down the throats of law-abiding citizens. Every minute of every day, the federal government encroaches on our privacy, undermining the constitutional rights of every American. But of course they eloquently defend their actions—claiming they do so in order to keep us safe (how sweet of them). Ronald Reagan once said, "I hope we have once again reminded people that man is not free unless government is limited. There's a clear cause and effect here that is as neat and predictable as a law of physics: as government expands, liberty contracts."[4]

If you think about it for a moment, the millennial generation (those persons born between 1984–2000) has not grown up with a self-governing model that is depicted in the Constitution. Government bureaucracy is what they know. Some would argue that the size and scope of government exploded after Reagan left office. Yet the point is that mainstream millennials are disgusted by the United States. But this is all trained behavior. Millennials have been raised under the philosophy and teaching of progressivism (this is not referring to Progressive Insurance, but to an ideology of replacing the Constitution with something new, for example).

Under the guidance of progressive teachers, young people are taught to believe it was American Imperialism that came to America and brutally murdered the Indians and stole their land. Under progressive teaching, young people are brainwashed to believe it was American Imperialism that forced its way into Africa, kidnapping thousands upon thousands of Africans, shipping them off to America as slaves. Under progressive education, young people are programmed to believe that the poverty in America, and even around the world, is caused by the crooked capitalists of Wall Street. (To get an image of this brand of thinking, just think back to the Occupy Wall Street protesters, holding signs like "People

Before Profit," "Smash Capitalism," and "We Are the 99 Percent." Yeah. We know. Unforgettable.)

Occupy Wall Street and other similar riots breaking out throughout America are all indicators of this growing anti-American movement. And it's not stopping anytime soon. It grows by the day—even by the incident. And most of these protesters who take to the streets are among the more than 80 million millennials who occupy American life. And yet the irony is that millennials, who have zero respect for their nation, wouldn't be able to do the things or have the things they do if it wasn't for the sacred freedoms they have as Americans. Which, again, this points back to the apathetic, ignorant, and deluded narcissistic Americans who are taking over.

From Occupy Wall Street comes Occupy Universities (#MillionStudentMarch), a rally of self-entitled college students who are demanding their right to freebies for life. And if they don't get what they want, well, then they'll just tweet out to all their friends to join them on campus as they protest and boycott until they get what they want. And what is it they want? They are demanding free-tuition colleges. They are also demanding that the $1.3 trillion student loan debt be wiped clean. And, if that were not enough, students are demanding the minimum wage be bumped up to $15.00 an hour.

Just like the signs of Occupy Wall Street, these entitled students are coming out in droves carrying signs, like "Degrees Not Receipts" and "Is This a School or a Corporation?" Since when did these students get off thinking they can demand such ridiculous handouts? Oh, yeah, we almost forgot—their entire lives have been, at least to some degree, lived on government handouts.

This generation has always been told they are winners, not losers (because we don't want to destroy their self-esteem); this generation is given passing grades (because there are no failures); this generation hasn't sacrificed a thing in life. To them, freedom is a guarantee, something that is easily taken for granted.

In the minds of this generation, America is only great if it pays for their education, health care, groceries, and most of their living expenses. But God forbid if these entitled students are expected to work hard to make money, or expected to pay for things they want, or even defend their rights to live freely. Again, apathy, ignorance, and narcissism have all been contributing factors to this entitlement mentality. But have these students even thought through who will pay for all of this free stuff? Do they realize that what they are demanding is utterly insane?

This growing anti-American movement has lived on government handouts for far too long. As government continues to grow, so does the people's dependency of it. In the era of entitlement, almost half of US households now receive some type of government handout, which is why America is referred to as the Welfare State. And this is the "America" this generation thinks our founders built.

Doesn't it trouble you that we are living in a time when more Americans rely on government handouts than ever before? And you know something else? Government handouts are not going to last. These entitlements that college students are demanding as their *human right* is not only economically destructive, but it poses a danger to our national security. Amassing more national debt so that college students can have free education is not feasible, constitutional, or even wise.

Unfortunately, America has now reached a tipping point. The growth of entitlement spending has now absorbed the entire US defense budget. That's almost $1 trillion! Talk about wasteful spending.

If Not America, Then Who?

To get right down to it, this anti-American brashness needs to answer a few important questions. First, if America isn't good for the world, then who or what is? Second, if America is no longer the superpower of the world, then what nation will take her place? And third, if America is no longer the superpower, then what immediate effects will that have around the world?

The truth is—and we're not ashamed to say this—America is good for the world. However, we would like to clarify that the America that we currently live in, at this time (shifting into a more corrupt faction), is definitely not the America of yesteryear. That is to say that America has become a danger to itself. And what we are trying to show this generation is that America wasn't meant to be the nation it is today. It is and was so much more.

America was built on a strong belief in God, and structured on a constitutional system to protect the equal rights of each and every citizen. Today, unfortunately, America has turned its back on God, making it more godless than ever before. In fact, did you know that millennials, who comprise the largest generation in American history, are the most godless America has ever seen? This is not really that surprising, is it?

The fastest growing religious movement among millennials isn't Christianity, Catholicism, or even Islam. Nope. It is the "nones." These are people who claim to have no religious ties whatsoever, and, frankly, they don't really care if they do or if they don't. This is the generation that is rising up in America today. They are the ones attending the universities, entering the workforce, and running for public office. And if you haven't noticed, millennials have little to no desire to get married and start a family.

To put it another way: the most godless generation in American history is gaining control—control over the media, control over politics, and control over commerce and business. Of course, we've already seen what a godless education system looks like. Just look at the Department of Indoctrination (excuse us ... we mean Education). However, this shouldn't come as a shock. Scripture repeatedly makes it clear. The psalmist declared, "Blessed is the nation whose God is the LORD, the people whom he has chosen as his heritage" (Psalm 33:12 ESV). And Isaiah said, "For the nation and kingdom that will not serve God shall perish; those nations shall be utterly laid waste" (Isaiah 60:12 ESV).

Not very long ago America was formed by immovable Christians—Christians who knew what they stood for and were willing to die for such shared beliefs. It was a nation founded on Judeo-Christian laws and principles, and a beacon of light to the rest of the world. Now, however, America doesn't know what it stands for. In a culture where everyone obsesses over their sexual and gender identity, it seems that America is having her own cultural identity crisis. She has always had the strongest national identity, which is an identity, according to Dennis Prager, that is made up of three pillars of Americanism: "Liberty," "In God We Trust," and "e pluribus unum," which is Latin for "out of many, one." But now Americans aren't taught these three pillars of Americanism at all. Rather, Americanism has been turned into nationalism, which is a growing movement to deconstruct the United States of America into a more Marxist view of a classless society.

This was put on worldwide display in 2011, when an issue of Action Comics depicted Superman renouncing his US citizenship, following a major clash with the federal government.[5] Up to that point, Superman had always been pro-America since his creation in 1938, a symbol of democracy and freedom. However, times have changed. Superman is no longer the patriotic hero we all grew up loving, especially to the older generation. The Superman for this new generation is more of a nationalist representing socialism.

In the issue, Superman conveys a message to the president, and thus to the entire world: "I intend to speak before the United Nations tomorrow and inform them that I am renouncing my U.S. citizenship. I'm tired of having my actions construed as instruments of U.S. policy. ... Truth, justice, and the American way ... it's not enough anymore."[6]

Despite the good America has done all over the world, the American way is no longer warranted (according to the left). Although Superman is of course a fictitious superhero, the message the liberal left is conveying through the Man of Steel is a prevailing one. It is a message that is taking hold of more and more Americans, and resonating with them. The message is loud and clear: America is no longer good for the world. Therefore, it needs to be reformed into something much different. And so they have.

Things Are Messed Up

It's pretty messed up when the Ten Commandments monuments are being evicted from their place of residence. It's pretty messed up when small-business owners (who happen to be Christian) are sued by same-sex couples for refusing to do something against their convictions. It's pretty messed up when people are silenced and ridiculed for voicing an opinion. And it's even more messed up that taxpayer dollars fund Planned Parenthood, which is an organization that dismembers unborn babies and sells their body parts to the highest bidder. It's more than messed up—it is detestable!

Who would have thought that America would become a nation trumpeting abortions, same-sex marriage, and euthanasia? Who would have ever thought the Socialist Party of America would have a chance at one of their candidates winning the presidency? Yet this is where we currently find America. Could you imagine how much worse it will get if commonsense Americans don't put a stop to this detestable government?

Get Connected

So far everything we have told you about this anti-American movement is true. We don't write this stuff to upset you or depress you, even though sometimes we do get very upset and depressed, I (Jason) more so than Alex. Rather, we write to make more people aware of how bad things are. But it doesn't just end there. As we explain how bad things are, we are reminded and encouraged that it just means there's more to be done.

You see, although things are looking bleak, there's still a remnant of fair-minded millennials who get it. They just need some guidance. As a matter of fact, what they need is you. That's what it's going to take. If you want to put an end to the despotism in America, all you have to do is reach millennials and plurals with the gospel of Jesus Christ. Every generation starting out can use some solid teachers and mentors, godly examples who can shape their young minds and guide them with wisdom and truth. Just as young Americans have been taught to believe a lie, so too can they be taught the truth. But who will do it? Who will teach them truth?

The bulk of education in America isn't teaching young people the truth, so enough is enough. Let's do something about it. The good news is that it has already started. There is a growing number of young people receiving education outside of the secularized educational system, and it's making a difference. Now it may be five to one, but at least there's a growing movement of families and local churches taking ownership in educating the next generation.

If we want to see more solutions to the problems plaguing America, let's focus our attention on three key challenges, which are three challenges we believe will change your life, and, Lord willing, will change America for the better.

Challenge #1: Discover Hope

First things first. Put aside a defeatist attitude and put on a victorious one. Be hopeful that America and the generation coming up aren't totally lost. There's still time. We don't know how much time until Christ returns, but let's not waste it by being a sour patch kid.

Too often, Christians sit around and complain just the same about how messed up things are, but that only makes matters worse. "Nones" are on the rise because not enough Christians live and preach the gospel to them. That may be an unsettling thing to hear, but it's the honest truth. Christians don't get a free pass on this. We are responsible, as ambassadors of Christ, to deliver and announce the message of the gospel. Paul listed a string of convicting questions in his epistle to the Romans: "How then will they call on him in whom they have not believed? And how are they to believe in him of whom they have never heard? And how are they to hear without someone preaching?" (Romans 10:14 ESV).

In my (Jason) travels around the country, I'm often asked if there's any hope for this generation. My answer every single time is *absolutely*! Lest we forget, Daniel 4:3 boldly declares, "How great are His signs, and how mighty are His wonders! His kingdom is an everlasting kingdom, and His dominion is from generation to generation" (NKJV). God is the God over each and every person, place, generation, and nation. Furthermore, although this generation is pretty messed up, they also have a ton of potential. But they need godly people who are willing to invest in them, to shape their lives so they can shape America for the better.

Just as you received the gospel and now live it, find hope in declaring it to this generation. Paul challenged Timothy, "Preach the word; be ready in season and out of season; reprove, rebuke, and exhort, with complete patience and teaching" (2 Timothy 4:2 ESV). This leads to our second challenge.

Challenge #2: Refocus Your Priorities

It's very important that you focus your attention, energy, and resources on this generation. We all know how lost this generation is, so let's focus our attention on getting millennials out of this mess. You may be thinking, *This sounds great, Jason and Alex, but no millennial is going to listen to me.* Well, you won't know unless you try.

The truth is that we have found that millennials actually love engaging older people. And they also respect their friends who are bold and articulate about what they believe. Sure, they love connecting with their friends on Facebook and Instagram, but they really love having meaningful conversations with people who care and want to have that kind of exchange with them. You might be a parent or grandparent, or perhaps a millennial yourself. Whatever the case, ask yourself, how do I want to make a difference in the lives of millennials?

To make a difference in the lives of millennials, or anyone for that matter, it requires cultivation, which takes time. And it takes a lot of intentionality and hard work too. So be patient. Remain focused and determined to cultivate relationships with this generation that is dying for authentic relationships. There are a ton of books, blogs, and videos about millennials. People label them as dejected, ignorant of the facts, and too distracted with their selfish lives to care about religion, politics, and family values. This may be true to some extent (definitely among "nones"), but why is that?

One huge reason is the breakdown of transferable faith from one generation to the next. To explain how this has happened, allow us to use a candy illustration. Now I (Jason) love candy, so this will be fun. Think of your favorite piece of candy for a moment. (I'm thinking of Reese's Peanut Butter Cups—yummy!) Now think of that candy in bite-sized form. If you are anything like me, I don't mess around with bite-size pieces (or minis). When I want Reese's® Peanut Butter Cups, I get the king size with four cups. Just ask my kids. They know their dad goes all out when it comes to candy.

Like bite-size candy, millennials have been given a form of

bite-size Christianity, which, as you can imagine, doesn't really satisfy. We open the Bible like a bag of candy, reach in and grab a few minis, and then toss a few small pieces in their mouths, as if that will satisfy their cravings. But all it really does is create a desire for more—that's it.

Young people aren't given any more, which has resulted in many bailing from the church. Or perhaps this explains why many stop listening to their parents about spiritual matters altogether. Why is this? It is because they were only given bite-size pieces of Christianity. Enough with this bite-size version of Jesus. We need to give millennials the whole bag of the gospel. Which brings us to our third challenge.

Challenge #3: Be a Model of Courage

In this section, we want to point out two men (in particular) who exemplify extraordinary courage: Patrick Henry and Alexander Hamilton.

Patrick Henry did something remarkable, something no one at the time was brave enough to do. He stood up in Virginia and declared freedom from the king, a declaration that many people said was treason. Despite the charge, however, Henry was not willing to back down from what he knew was right. He knew freedom for all Americans meant treason in the eyes of an evil ruler. And if he didn't stand up and fight against such evil oppression, then all hope of freedom would be lost. Patrick Henry is a model of extraordinary courage—one not only to remember but to emulate in the bleak days we are living in right now.

The other brave soul was the legendary Alexander Hamilton. Hamilton was not only brilliant, but he was also astute. For instance, Hamilton saw the coming destruction of America in his time. Rather than sit idly by, however, he did something about it. He could have easily ignored the threats his nation faced, yet because of his boldness and unwillingness to see chaos and corruption breed, Hamilton demanded a Constitutional Convention in Philadelphia with delegates from each colony. It was at the Convention that the Constitution of the United States emerged, thus establishing a newfound government that not only saved America but ushered in the greatest nation in all of history—thanks in large part to the brave leadership of Alexander Hamilton.

Patrick Henry and Alexander Hamilton are just two examples of the courage and bravery of our founders. Our founders lived with a strong belief in God, they built a nation established on absolute truth, and they ordained standards of morality, ethics, and values by which to live. Our forefathers sacrificed their lives, fortunes, and sacred honor to establish a republic that would champion these great ideals.

The key is that our founders were brave enough to do something greater than themselves. George Washington was willing to die in battle in hopes that America might be free. Patrick Henry was willing to be hung for treason in order to awaken an army of courageous Americans to finally break free from evil dictatorship. And Alexander Hamilton was willing to lose his livelihood in order to establish a government that would ensure the prosperity of future generations.

Imagine if the courage of these great men of valor infected Christians all across the United States in our own day and time. Just imagine what would happen if courage, bravery, and sacrifice exploded in churches all over America. God is awakening many Christians to be courageous once again—to stand for what is right (like Patrick Henry), and to be willing to sacrifice whatever necessary (like Alexander Hamilton). As you finish this chapter, here's a challenging question for you to honestly answer: what is preventing *you* from being a brave Christian who will stand and do what is right?

Stand Strong: Truth

All this talk and demand for the government to give out free stuff is symptomatic of a greater problem. This generation has come to believe that bigger government is a good thing. Just imagine a government big enough and powerful enough to make all your dreams come true. No more debt. No more having to work hard and try and earn your way to the top. Sounds pretty awesome, right?

Wrong. The truth is that this generation is not living in reality. Reliance on government to take care of your problems goes far deeper than laziness and entitlement. It points to a need for God. All of these boycotts, riots, marches, and walk-outs that are taking place around the country are demonstrations of the inner struggle Americans are having. They are struggling to be loved. To be forgiven.

No amount of money or power from the federal government can wipe away the debt, inequality, and depravity in our country. Everything this generation is trying to do apart from God will never work. Jesus is the answer, not government.

Be that voice of truth to this generation. As they seek for a bigger government to solve all of their problems, point them back to Jesus Christ who gave up His life so that they can have eternal life with Him (John 17:3; 1 John 5:10–12).

CHAPTER 10

THE COURTS
AND CHRISTIANITY

*Of the many influences that have shaped
the United States into a distinctive nation and people,
none may be said to be more fundamental
and enduring than the Bible.*[1]

—RONALD REAGAN

The US Supreme Court stands as the final ruling body regarding the interpretation of American law. In recent years, concerns have been raised regarding the "activism" of the Supreme Court as it has increasingly interpreted cases to make laws that our Constitution did not include and that our nation's founders did not have in mind. The concepts of "authorial intent" (which is interpreting cases based on what the Constitution originally intended) and constitutional law are increasingly shifting to case law or what some call "judiciary legislation" (which are laws created as the result of a judiciary decision).

Yet this has not always been the case. As the Supreme Court began to hand down judicial decisions, the earlier courts recognized the biblical basis for America's ideals, and for a time the Supreme Court labored to uphold this intent. For example, a court decision in the US Supreme Court in 1892 stated, "No purpose of action against religion can be imputed to any legislation, state or national, because this is a religious people. ... This is a Christian nation." The court cited eighty-seven different historical precedents to support that America was Christian in its founding, principles, and intents.[2]

Don't interfere with anything in the Constitution. That must be maintained, for it is the only safeguard of our liberties.[3]
—*Abraham Lincoln*

Justice Earl Warren, a former US Supreme Court Chief Justice, shared in a *Time* magazine interview in 1954:

I believe that no one can read the history of our country, without realizing the Good Book, and the Spirit of the Savior, which have, from the beginning, been our guiding genius. Whether we look at the first Charter of Virginia, or the Charter of New England, or the Charter of Massachusetts Bay, or the Fundamental Orders of Connecticut, the same objective is present, a Christian land governed by Christian principles.

I believe the entire Bill of Rights came into being because of the knowledge our forefathers had of the Bible and a belief in it. Freedom of belief, of expression, of assembly, of petition, the dignity of the individual, the sanctity of the home, equal justice under the law, and the reservation of the people, I would like to believe that we are living today in the Spirit of the Christian religion. I would also like to believe long as we do, no great harm can come to our country.[4]

Did the Ten Commandments Influence America's Founders?

The influence of the Ten Commandments, found in the Old Testament, on America's history and laws is a powerful testimony regarding Christianity's role in our nation. But many secularist websites deny that Christianity or even a minimalist belief in natural law (for examaple, the Ten Commandments) influenced the founders at all. But consider the words of Noah Webster, one of the men who participated in the writing of the US Constitution. Webster asserted, "It is the sincere desire of the writer that our citizens should early understand that the genuine source of correct republican principles is the Bible, particularly the New Testament or the Christian religion."[5]

Webster went on to write in his 1823 work, *Letters to a Young Gentleman*, "The duties of man are summarily comprised in the Ten Commandments, consisting of two tables; one comprehending the duties which we owe immediately to God—the other, the duties we owe to our fellow man."[6] It is clearly evident that he understood the Bible's influence on law and citizenship. Again, remember that this man helped write our Constitution.

John Quincy Adams, our nation's sixth president, also spoke regarding the role of the Decalogue in the nation's founding:

> It pleased God to deliver on Mount Sinai a compendium of His holy law and to write it with His own hand on durable tables of stone. This law, which is commonly called the Ten Commandments or Decalogue ... is immutable and universally obligatory ... and was incorporated into the judicial law.[7]

And as recently as 1950, the Florida Supreme Court continued to refer to the Ten Commandments as an important source of our nation's laws, stating:

> A people unschooled about the Sovereignty of God, the Ten Commandments, the ethics of Jesus, could never have evolved the Bill of Rights, the Declaration of Independence, and the Constitution. There is not one solitary fundamental principle of our democratic policy that did not stem directly from the basic moral concepts as embodied in the Decalogue.[8]

Natural Law versus Case Law

Often dismissed today in this conversation is that US constitutional law recognizes the value of natural law, as does the Bill of Rights and many of America's constitutional amendments. For example, Amendments 13 through 15 banned slavery and recognized the Constitution's statements of life and liberty extending to all African Americans.

In more recent times, however, case law has increasingly taken precedence over the influence of natural law in American courts. Space does not allow the ability to fully address this issue, but we want to mention some of what could be considered the "worst" legal decisions based on case law rather than natural law.

Slavery

Perhaps the best-known case is *Dred Scott v. Sanford* in 1857. Dred Scott was a slave who sued for his freedom when his master moved from a free state to Missouri, which was then a slave state. He argued from the legal principle "once free, always free." According to writer Brian Duignan,

"Free negro[es] of the African race" were not then and *could never be* U.S. citizens, according to Taney. Rather than simply dismissing the case as improvidently granted, however, Taney took it upon himself to resolve the country's Sectional Crisis by declaring unconstitutional the Missouri Compromise (1820)—which had prohibited slavery in the Louisiana Purchase (except Missouri) north of 36°30'—and the Kansas-Nebraska Act (1854)—which had allowed the residents of Kansas and Nebraska to decide whether their territories would be free or slave—on the grounds that any prohibition of slavery would violate the Fifth Amendment right of slaveholders not to be deprived of their "property" without due process of law. Taney thus effectively established the legality of slavery throughout the United States.

The decision understandably outraged anti-slavery forces in the North and emboldened pro-slavery forces in the South. Far from resolving the Sectional Crisis, Taney made it much worse. The eventual result? The Civil War.[9]

Child Labor Exploitation

A lesser-known yet important case was *Hammer v. Dagenhart* in 1918. In this 5–4 Supreme Court decision, it ruled that Congress lacked the power to regulate *against* child labor through its authority to regulate interstate commerce. Creating a distinction between "commerce" and "manufacturing," as well as the meaning of "regulation," the Court stated, "The power is one to control the means by which commerce is carried on, which is directly the contrary of the assumed right to forbid commerce from moving, and thus destroy it as to particular commodities."[10] The result of this case law ruling was the ability of factories and mines to continue labor exploitation of children until 1941, when the ruling was eventually overturned in *United States v. Darby Lumber Co.*

Japanese American Internment Camps

In 1944, our own US Supreme Court ruled 6–3 to endorse the forced relocation of Japanese Americans to internment camps. Why? Case law. Rather than an appeal to the legal rights of all Americans that "all men are created equal," the Court referred to case law to declare:

Compulsory exclusion of large groups of citizens from their homes, except under circumstances of direst emergency and peril, is inconsistent with our basic governmental institutions. But when, under conditions of modern warfare, our shores are threatened by hostile forces, the power to protect must be commensurate with the threatened danger.[11]

This racist act led to the extreme mistreatment of many Japanese Americans along the West Coast of the United States simply based on their background rather than any crime that had been committed.

Same-Sex Marriage

Most recently, on June 26, 2015, the US Supreme Court also referred to case law to redefine the definition of marriage across America. Rather than affirming natural law, Justice Kennedy noted in his opinion for the Court that marriage is an institution that "has evolved over time." Instead of noting a clear distinction between the relationship held between a man and woman in marriage, and two men or two women in a committed relationship, the Court argued the "right to marry" is a fundamental right that applies to both same and opposite sex partnerships.

However, this decision was based merely on case law, not a clear constitutional law nor on the basis of natural law. This decision is having and will have dire consequences on our nation in a variety of ways, the most important of which will include blurring the distinctions that define a family unit, leaving the door open to still "other forms" or marriage (polygamy, incest, or other forms), and legal persecution toward those with religious convictions that oppose the redefinition of marriage.

This third concern is already taking place. The case of Kentucky clerk Kim Davis dominated headlines in 2015 and has become well known. She refused to offer marriage licenses when this law was changed, eventually being arrested for a time as a result. Many less visible attacks are also taking place, which include local churches and issues related to church membership and marriage, Christian-owned businesses that choose not to participate with same-sex marriages, any Christian agency that deals with adoptions, Christian schools and colleges, employment policies in Christian nonprofits and businesses, and similar areas. The bottom line is that case law is trumping natural law and the end result is increased hostility toward those who seek to live a biblical worldview.

The Bible supports polygamy, rape, and incest, so the traditional model of marriage between one man and one woman is not really the biblical model. This argument has become popular recently as critics have sought to attack traditional family in America. Those who take support in this claim miss what the Bible actually teaches regarding this issue. In fact, Jesus taught that marriage was always intended to be between one man and one woman (Matthew 19:4–6).

At this point, the critic is quick to point out that Solomon had hundreds of wives and concubines, Abraham had a child with a servant, and so forth. The sections of the Bible that record these incidents are called historical narrative. In other words, the Bible is not condoning the actions of these individuals, but is reporting what actually happened.

"God Is Not Fixing This"

Following the terrorist attacks in San Bernardino, California, in 2015, the front page of the *New York Daily News* declared, "God is not fixing this." This headline referred to the observation that despite the many people who claim their "thoughts and prayers" are with someone after a tragedy, God was not intervening to help in the increase of violence and mass shootings in America.

But what do we expect? In many ways, America has already turned its back on God. Furthermore, prayer to almighty God is a serious act. Just because we don't live in a peaceful world doesn't mean that God isn't listening to our prayers. We live in a fallen world where bad things happen every day, whether mass shootings or other forms of suffering, such as cancer or miscarriages. It is a myth that God would give us everything we ask for in life.

We also need God's protection. The increasing bloodshed on American soil will continue until we genuinely turn back to God. Our leaders must promote morality, natural law, and the Ten Commandments once again. We can follow God's precepts in our leadership, or continue to fight truth and refuse to acknowledge the reality that our world is lost without God. Will we humble our hearts or harden our hearts?

God's Word Can Still Influence Our Nation

It was not the words of an early American, but rather a more recent presidential voice that offered encouragement in recent reflection on the Bible's influence in our country. President Ronald Reagan offered these words of encouragement that continue to ring true today for those who seek to see Scripture influence our nation once again:

> The Bible and its teachings helped form the basis for the Founding Fathers' abiding belief in the inalienable rights of the individual, rights which they found implicit in the Bible's teachings of the inherent worth and dignity of each individual. This same sense of man patterned the convictions of those who framed the English system of law inherited by our own Nation, as well as the ideals set forth in the Declaration of Independence and the Constitution.[12]

In a recent event I (Alex) was privileged to emcee in Raleigh, North Carolina, where approximately ten-thousand Americans attended a We Stand with God rally. The event included a thousand-voice choir, several ministers, and a speech by Arkansas governor and Republican presidential candidate Mike Huckabee. As I opened our event together, God brought to mind Proverbs

14:34. So I shared these words with the audience: "Righteousness exalts a nation, but sin is a reproach to any people" (ESV).

These biblical words were not intended to disrespect the crowd, but were focused on encouraging Americans to seek God's righteousness and His ways in a time in which darkness has turned many areas of our nation to reproach or a detriment. God's Word helped make America strong, and God's Word can help make our nation great once again. Our ultimate concern is not whether or not our courtrooms display Scripture, but whether or not our lives reflect it.

Let us wrap up this chapter with the powerful words of James 1:22: "Do not merely listen to the word, and so deceive yourselves. Do what it says." Did you catch that? If we only listen to God's truth, we can be deceived. The Bible was not designed only to be read or honored in our nation. It was given to be applied to our day-to-day lives.

I saw that the most important thing I had to do was to give myself to the reading of the Word of God, and to meditation on it. . . . What is the food of the inner man? Not prayer, but the Word of God; and . . . not the simple reading of the Word of God, so that it only passes through our minds, just as water runs through a pipe, but considering what we read, pondering over it, and applying it to our hearts.[13]
—*George Müller*

We can't make our courts or Congress or president obey God's principles, but we can focus on living out God's teachings in our own lives. When we learn and live what we believe, we offer powerful evidence that God's Word is true. Jesus taught long ago, "Let your light shine before others, that they may see your good deeds and glorify your Father in heaven" (Matthew 5:16). Our work and our words combine for a powerful witness. In this same passage,

Jesus also taught that a city that is set on a hill cannot be hidden (v. 14). And in 1630, the passengers of the *Arabella* left England for America using this same verse. John Winthrop noted:

> For we must consider that we shall be as a city upon a hill, the eyes of all people are upon us; so that if we shall deal falsely with our God in this work we have undertaken, and so cause Him to withdraw His present help from us, we shall shame the faces of many of God's worthy servants, and cause their prayers to be turned into curses.[14]

These passengers became part of what became known as the Great Migration to America, where almost fourteen thousand more Puritans came to Massachusetts. By 1636, just six years later, this same movement led to the creation of Harvard University, developed for the purpose of training Puritan ministers.

Still today, we have the opportunity to be a city on a hill. It begins in our own lives, extends to our families, and reaches beyond us and into our communities and nation. We can see America stand strong once again. It will take the commitment of every Christian to pray, to prepare, and to pursue a life that honors God and impacts others—but it can be great once again.

CHAPTER 11

WAKE UP, CHURCH

Who will rise up for me against the wicked?
Who will take a stand for me against evildoers?
—PSALM 94:16

A firestorm of controversy hit when a hacking group accessed over 40 million private subscribers on Ashley Madison, an online service to help married couples fulfill their fantasies by committing adultery. Their motto is, "Life is short. Have an affair." Many were shocked to find a spouse, a friend, a colleague, or even their pastor on the naughty list. As a result, shock, disappointment, sadness, and anger were all emotions many have had to deal with through the painful revelation leaked to the public.

However, there was one particular name no one expected to find: Josh Duggar, from the TLC show *19 Kids and Counting*. After being exposed, Josh released this opening statement: "I have been the biggest hypocrite ever. While espousing faith and family values, I have secretly over the last several years been viewing pornography on the internet and this became a secret addiction and I became unfaithful to my wife."[1]

In one week alone, Ed Stetzer reported that over four hundred pastors, elders, and deacons throughout America resigned from leadership positions because they were having secret affairs through the services of Ashley Madison. Tragically, a pastor and professor of a leading seminary took his own life after his name was leaked to the public. He left behind a loving wife and two grown children.

These are real people, and they have real problems. Our hearts break for leaders caught in sexual sin, and we grieve for their families. We can only imagine the guilt, despair, and shame that floods the souls of pastors caught in the bondage of adultery.

Sexual Sin

Throughout our speaking travels, we talk with pastors of every background and denomination. We can't tell you how many pastors struggle with depression and sexual sin. With the job comes endless requests from church members, nonstop committee meetings, and high demands from elders and deacons. All of this explains the fatigue, burnout, and nervous breakdowns experienced by many pastors.

But as the pressure rises, many pastors don't know how to deal with it. Most stuff it down, staying busy doing ministry and trying hard to ignore the symptoms. But as the pressure intensifies, instead of turning to Jesus Christ, these well-intentioned pastors turn to sexual sin instead. This doesn't explain, nor does it excuse, their sexual behavior. Adultery is morally wrong. It is a sin against a holy God, and the people committing this immoral act need to be removed from their post, which seldom happens. It seems at times that some churches would much rather turn a blind eye than confront their pastor committing adultery.

However, we can't expect God to heal our land or to bless our churches as long as we have pastors who are in sexual sin leading the church. Hebrews 13:4 reads, "Let marriage be held in honor among all, and let the marriage bed be undefiled, for God will judge the sexually immoral and adulterous" (ESV). And Solomon puts it directly when he writes, "He who commits adultery lacks sense; he who does it destroys himself" (Proverbs 6:32 ESV). Based on Hebrews 13:4 and Proverbs 6:23, anyone committing adultery is defiled, lacks wisdom, and is living a life of destruction. Their sin will not only destroy their lives, but the lives of their families as well. And how much more so with a pastor?

The Bible pointedly states, "For if someone does not know how to manage his own household, how will he care for God's church?" (1 Timothy 3:5 ESV). The reason is sound. If a leader can't manage his own home, then he is unfit to lead a church. Therefore, if a pastor is committing adultery, it's safe to say—according to the Word of God—he isn't qualified to lead a church.

It is important that we don't overlook this. There have been too many cases where the church didn't confront the situation they were presented with. For whatever reason, most churches don't want to address the topic of sexual sin. And so the pastor continues to sin, and leads that church in sin. This is simply wrong, and it has to stop.

Ultimately, these pastors are responsible before the Lord for their own actions. They know that their sexual sin is morally wrong and that someday, in the not-too-distant future, they will stand before Jesus to give an account of how they lived their life. However, this doesn't get church leaders and members off the hook. There is a level of accountability that people within the church need to own up to. And that is holiness.

In a sexually heightened society, Paul encouraged the church in Corinth with these words: "Since we have these promises, beloved, let us cleanse ourselves from every defilement of body and spirit, bringing holiness to completion in the fear of God" (2 Corinthians 7:1 ESV). It is we, the church, who are responsible to help one another not to defile our bodies, but together we are to pursue and fulfill holiness in the fear of God. This will never happen as long as churches turn a blind eye to the sexual sin pervading pastors.

Compromised Church

Another sin destroying the church is that of compromise. The kind of compromise we're talking about here is the gradual retreat from the truth. The senior demon in C. S. Lewis' classic book *The Screwtape Letters*, named Screwtape, made these remarks about compromise: "Indeed the safest road to Hell is the gradual one— the gentle slope, soft underfoot, without sudden turnings, without milestones, without signposts."[2] The point is that a little bit of com- promise eventually leads to total rejection. What was good is now evil, and what was evil is now good (Isaiah 5:20).

And it is this kind of compromise that is unfolding before our very eyes. The church is the "pillar of truth" (1 Timothy 3:15), yet sadly many within the church have turned them into "pillars of political correctness." What the Bible unequivocally calls sin (e.g., abortion, same-sex marriage, adultery, lying, stealing, etc.) is now a matter of personal opinion.

Likewise, the policy of political correctness has also "corrected" absolute statements that are offensive, or statements that may make people feel uncomfortable in church—statements like, "Jesus is the only way," "People are sinners," and "The Bible is the Word of God." So they compromise by changing these "intolerant" statements into something more tolerated and accepted: "Jesus is *a* way," "People aren't sinners; they just make bad choices sometimes," and "The Bible contains some good lessons by which to live."

Enough with being politically correct in the church. The Word of God has no interest in popularity, likeability, or being politically correct. Could you imagine if Moses, Joseph, Esther, Nehemiah, or Paul were politically correct? Not a chance! As Christians, we are not called to political correctness, but to correct the dogmatic nonsense destroying our nation. Jesus said, "You will be hated by everyone because of me" (Matthew 10:22).

In today's secularized church, it's unpopular to preach about sin. It's unpopular to believe in hell. It's unpopular to hold to truth. How has this happened? How does a church go from teaching the Word of God to censoring it? It is quite simple really. It starts with wanting to be popular with the culture. Desire turns into acceptance, acceptance turns into accommodation, and, before you know it, you have a big church filled with a bunch of nonbelievers following a false teacher—a false teacher who supplements God's truth for man's truth, a false teacher who tells his people to follow their heart and pursue happiness.

Once again, lest we forget, compromising the Word of God in the church is a mockery to God. The apostle Paul lays down some strict words for leaders in the church. He charged Timothy:

> Do not be ashamed of the testimony about our Lord, nor of me his prisoner, but share in suffering for the gospel by the power of God, who saved us and called us to a holy calling, not because of our works but because of his own purpose and grace, which he gave us in Christ Jesus before the ages began, and which now has been manifested through the appearing of our Savior Christ Jesus, who abolished death and brought life and immortality to light through the gospel. (2 Timothy 1:8–10 ESV)

Paul is essentially reminding pastors, and thus all Christians, that the church doesn't belong to humans. Church leaders don't own the church; they are simply servants charged to care for the needs of the church.

It is Jesus Christ who is the Head of the church, it was Jesus Christ who gave up His life to redeem a people to a holy calling, and it is Jesus Christ who charges leaders throughout the church to not be ashamed of His testimony. Rather, they are to preach the manifestation, proclamation, and resurrection of Jesus Christ without compromise.

You may be thinking, *What do I do? I'm not a pastor or even a church leader. I'm just a member trying to do what's right for my family.* First, you are more than just a member—you are of the royal priesthood of God (1 Peter 2:9). Second, you are a child of God possessed with gifts of the Holy Spirit. Third, you have a special calling to lead and disciple others in your sphere of influence for Christ. Fourth, God has placed you in the church you are in for a reason, so if you haven't figured out why that is, then do what's necessary to get with the program.

On the flip side, if you attend a compromised church, then you need to find a different church. Don't be involved in a church that pretends to honor the Word of God, when it really doesn't. Remember that what the church believes about the Bible, as well as how it preaches and lives out the Bible, tells a person everything they need to know about that particular church. It isn't to be measured by the vision of the pastor, the style of worship, or the programs it offers; rather, the church is a place for Christians to gather to worship Jesus Christ, equip the saints in the Word of God, and send them out to make disciples of all nations.

After one of our Stand Strong tours, a young couple came up to me (Jason) seeking some advice. They shared that they had some major concerns with what their pastor was teaching. I asked if they had done anything about it, like talk with the pastor about his doctrinal errors. They said they hadn't. When I asked if they were still attending the church, they said they still were. So I encouraged them to set up an appointment with the pastor.

They really didn't like that idea at all. They stressed that they weren't leaders in the church, so they didn't feel that was appropriate. Because of their response, I felt the need to challenge them that if their pastor was in fact falsely teaching from the Bible, then it was their responsibility to address it with him. If and when they do, they are to make sure their approach is with a pure heart, a good conscience, and with a sincere faith (1 Timothy 1:5; see also

Ephesians 4:15). They agreed. However, they weren't willing to confront the pastor at the risk of leaving the church.

This conversation with the young couple is very common. It is a conversation we are all too familiar with. We hear from plenty of frustrated Christians all across America, but not many of whom are willing to confront what is being taught from the pulpit Sunday after Sunday.

Comfortable and Bored

Christians have gotten too comfortable. They come to church for sixty minutes, and then go back to their busy lives. Church has become just an afterthought. But guess what? Comfortable Christians can lead to compromised churches. Pastors aren't the only ones to blame for leading churches astray. Complacent Christians play a big role in contributing to compromise as well.

The bottom line is that the American church needs to forfeit human compromises for the promises of God. Chasing what is trendy or following another celebrity pastor won't have a great impact on the coming generations. But getting back to Bible basics and teaching people core theology that is built around a discipleship model will impact the church greatly.

Do Your Job

Bill Belichick has won four Super Bowls and holds several records in the NFL. He's a legendary coach with a simple philosophy, "Do your job." Seems pretty simple, right? Well, it is. But do you want to know something? The same applies to church leaders too (even more so). As a pastor, I (Jason) have been there—through the ends and outs—and truth be told, church life hasn't been easy. But I do the job God has entrusted me to do, and it's very rewarding.

There are more than a few church leaders who aren't doing their job. They would rather hide out in their plush offices, appearing to do a job, when in reality their positions are producing very little. Take, for instance, this poll conducted by The Pew Forum on Religion and Public Life. What they discovered was that evangelical ministers from the United States reported a greater loss of influence than church leaders from any other country. Some 82 percent indicated that their movement was losing ground.

That means that churches in America are at an all-time low. Americans aren't attending churches because a majority think it has little relevance in their lives. This isn't good news at all. But it does speak to the growing problem of church leaders not doing their job. This reminds us of a hip-hop song by Lecrae called "Go Hard." In one of the verses of the song it says,

> Can they tell you value Jesus by the way you rep his name?
> Man, what's the point of living if I'm living for myself.
> Lord, empty out my life before I put you on the shelf.

The song is an ultimatum. You either *go hard* for Jesus, or you *go home.*

When Christians go hard for Jesus, the world is transformed by the gospel. But when Christians go home, the church is conformed by the culture. That is to say that when the church ceases to be what it was intended by God to be, then the culture will eventually swing to the dark side (had to throw *Star Wars* in here).

Top Twelve Issues the Church Wants to Hear

Now this may come as a shock, but as you read through the survey conducted by the preeminent Christian pollster George Barna, we think the findings will excite you. Barna conducted a survey of moderate to conservative churchgoers and asked what they would like to hear and learn from the pulpit. The results were as follows:

1. Abortion: beginning of life, right to life, contraception, adoption, and unwed mothers—91 percent

2. Religious persecution/liberty: personal duty, governmental duty, church response, global conditions—86 percent
3. Poverty: personal duty, government role, church role, homelessness, hunger, dependency—85 percent
4. Cultural restoration: appropriate morals, law and order, defensible values and norms, self-government—83 percent
5. Sexual identity: same-sex marriage, transgenderism, marriage, LGBT—82 percent
6. Israel: its role in the world, Christian responsibility to Israel, US foreign policy toward Israel and its enemies—80 percent
7. Christian heritage: the role of Christian faith in American history, the church's role in US development, modern-day relevance—79 percent
8. Role of government: biblical view, church-state relationship, personal responsibility, limitations—76 percent
9. Bioethics: cloning, euthanasia, genetic engineering, cryogenics, organ donation, surrogacy—76 percent
10. Self-governance: biblical support, personal conduct, impact on freedom, national sovereignty—75 percent
11. Church in politics/government: separation of church and state, legal boundaries, church resistance to government—73 percent
12. Islam: core beliefs, response to Islamic aggression, threat to US peace and domestic stability—72 percent[3]

This is great news indeed. Based on these findings, it seems there are still churchgoers who want to be informed and desire to make a difference in the world in which they live. So how do you get your pastor, who is not currently touching on these issues, to start doing his job and to start talking about these issues?

Well, for starters, it is our desire that you pray for your leadership and church. Next, you can set up a meeting with your pastor, take this survey with you, and encourage him to teach on several of these issues. Make sure you give him a copy of *Stand Strong America* as well. And last, be available to teach or invest in a group of instructors who are capable of teaching through this book at church. The facts don't lie. Simply by taking the time to show your pastor the truth that your church really does want him to teach on these issues will hopefully inspire him to do his job. Let that be our prayer.

#LeadLikeJesus

To see the church regain its position of authority in America, church leaders need to lead with godliness. They need to hold fast to the gospel—without compromise and without any trace of complacency. There's no shortage of bright, intelligent, and likeable pastors in America today. Churches are actually filled with them. But what the church in America really lacks is servant leaders.

Servant leaders are those who care more about others than they do about themselves. We often hear church members say, "Yeah, we know the pastor is pretty cocky and all, but hey, look at the size of the church. God is really using him!" But let's pause for a moment and think about Jesus. How did He lead? How did Jesus teach the people?

Jesus led by serving. He said He didn't come to be served, but to serve and to give His life for many (Matthew 20:28). Jesus said that He came to help the sick, which is something He demonstrated over and over again. He visited people no one wanted to visit. He spoke to people no one wanted to speak to. He touched people no one wanted to touch. And why did Jesus do this? He said, "For I have come down from heaven, not to do my own will but the will of him who sent me" (John 6:38 ESV). Jesus demonstrated unconditional love by taking the sins of humankind and dying on the cross. That's servant leadership.

A LEADER

1. A leader who stands up for biblical truth glorifies God (1 Corinthians 10:31).
2. A leader who stands up for biblical truth preaches the gospel of Jesus Christ (Romans 1:16).
3. A leader who stands up for biblical truth defends the Word of God (1 Peter 3:15–16).
4. A leader who stands up for biblical truth makes disciples (Matthew 28:19–20).
5. A leader who stands up for biblical truth loves others (Romans 12:10).
6. A leader who stands up for biblical truth protects life (Psalm 139).
7. A leader who stands up for biblical truth preserves freedom (Galatians 5).
8. A leader who stands up for biblical truth helps the poor (Luke 14:12–14).
9. A leader who stands up for biblical truth stands up for what is right (Romans 12:21).
10. A leader who stands up for biblical truth strengthens the church (Acts 14:21–23).

In the church culture today, we've become so enamored by the *personality* of the pastor that we've neglected the *person* of Jesus Christ. We've overlooked the pride of the pastor at the cost of neglecting humility, which is a quality every leader of a church needs.

Nowadays, pastors are trying to do it all. They are trying to preach every Sunday, expand their church programs, go to a multi-satellite model, write books, and get on a speaking circuit. However, all of this is in vain if they are not modeling a ministry after Jesus. Acts 20:28 reads, "Pay careful attention to yourselves and to all the flock, in which the Holy Spirit has made you overseers, to care for the church of God, which he obtained with his own blood" (ESV). The primacy of a leader, however, is to shepherd, to look after and care for his people. Ask yourself what kind of leader or pastor you are under right now. Would you say you attend an egocentric church or a Christ-centered church?

We are beginning to see a major shift taking place around the country. More families are leaving *egocentric* churches and taking refuge in *Christ-centered* churches. This is a good thing. We need to see more of this. So pray that the Holy Spirit will raise up true shepherds who will love and care for His people. Pray also that more families will find a loving church that exemplifies the grace and truth of Jesus Christ.

STAND STRONG: HUMILITY

The early church didn't spread because of a pastor, and it certainly didn't spread because of compromise. The church expanded, even in the harshest of conditions, because of the obedient faith of its devoted followers. The apostles, and many early church leaders, preached the gospel boldly in the midst of persecution. They were not only bold, but they were humble servants of God too.

The church was full of men like John the Baptist, who called out the sin of the king, and people like Mordecai and Esther, who risked their own lives for the safety of their people. Noah stood for righteousness in the midst of a corrupt world (Genesis 7:1), and Joseph stood for purity and resisted the temptations of the world (39:2–5). Jeremiah stood for justice and remained faithful against the opposition (Jeremiah 11:9–12), while Peter stood for truth and shepherded the church despite massive persecution.

CHAPTER 12

YOUR ROLE IN RESTORING AMERICA'S TRUE GREATNESS

Without God there is no virtue because
there is no prompting of the conscience ...
without God there is a coarsening of the society;
without God democracy will not and cannot
long endure. ... America needs God more than
God needs America. If we ever forget that
we are One Nation Under God,
then we will be a Nation gone under.[1]

—RONALD WILSON REAGAN

America clearly rests upon a strong Christian heritage. Certain individuals in American history, such as Christopher Columbus, even believed that America was a nation in covenant with God. Regardless of how contemporary atheists or critics seek to revise American history, it is undeniable that the nation was founded with a belief in a creator God and upon many biblical principles.

Even into the twentieth century we find American presidents affirming this view. President Woodrow Wilson noted in a popular speech, for instance, that "America was born a Christian nation. America was born to exemplify that devotion to the elements of righteousness which are derived from the revelations of Holy Scriptures."[2] And a close look at the Declaration of Independence,

US Constitution, Bill of Rights, and other important early legal documents of the nation clearly acknowledged God's existence and the Bible's influence.

Yet much has changed since the nation's founding. America's godly foundations continue to shift toward a growing violation against the views most of our nation's founders had about God. Ten important areas in the past half-century where this has shifted include:

1. Prohibiting Scripture reading in public schools (1962 Supreme Court decision);
2. Prohibiting prayer in public schools (1963 Supreme Court decision);
3. Prohibiting manger scenes and other religious displays in public areas;
4. Prohibiting the posting of the Ten Commandments in schools and in public buildings;
5. Prohibiting the teaching of God's creation in public schools alongside the teaching of evolution (Arkansas Supreme Court);
6. Legalizing abortion, the taking of unborn life (*Roe v. Wade*, 1973 Supreme Court decision);
7. Increased sexual immorality, as seen in mass numbers of divorces, rampant adultery, premarital sex, acceptance of same-sex relationships, and a rise in sexual abuse and pornography;
8. Increasingly turning away from the recognition of any Christian influence on national holidays (the use of Christian symbols and Christian worship is being minimized or prohibited, and meanwhile, secularism and pluralistic religions that incorporate New Age rituals, Native American spirituality, Islamic rituals, and other practices are allowed, endorsed, and even encouraged);

9. The redefinition of family and marriage to include two men or two women as married partners (2015 Supreme Court decision); and
10. The ongoing battle to privatize religious expression and punish those who stand for biblical convictions in schools, the workplace, and in the government.

Yet despite these disturbing concerns, we believe hope still remains for our nation. America is unique in that the components of our current government were intentionally organized in light of biblical concepts. For example, the concept of the three branches of government have their root in Isaiah 33:22, our nation's separation of powers was inspired by Jeremiah 17:9, and even the tax-exemption of churches was inspired by Ezra 7:24. It is no wonder the eighteenth president, Ulysses S. Grant, shared, "The Bible is the anchor of our liberties."[3]

Influencing Godly Change

At the very same prayer gathering at which our fortieth President Ronald Reagan warned that without God we would be "one Nation gone under," he said, "I believe that faith and religion play a critical role in the political life of our nation, and always has, and that the church—and by that I mean all churches, all denominations—has had a strong influence on the state, and this has worked to our benefit as a nation."[4] So what happens to America if we who are people of faith do not act—if we fail to stay engaged in our society? We further the rise of evil and immorality in our nation. In contrast, God calls us to rise up and implement our convictions in ways that can improve our communities and our country.

Let us share three important principles that can drive our personal response to helping America stand strong in this day: determination, investment, and conviction.

Determination: I Will Purpose in My Heart

Scripture is clear that God draws near to us when we draw near to Him (James 4:8). In 2 Chronicles 7:14, God told Israel these words that can also impact our nation if we will heed what He said: "If my people, who are called by my name, will humble themselves and pray and seek my face and turn from their wicked ways, then I will hear from heaven, and I will forgive their sin and will heal their land."

President Abraham Lincoln took such words to heart during his presidency. In a proclamation for a National Day of Prayer, he wrote:

> We have grown in numbers, wealth and power as no other nation has ever grown. But we have forgotten God. We have forgotten the gracious hand which preserved us in peace and multiplied and enriched and strengthened us; and we have vainly imagined, in the deceitfulness of our hearts, that all these blessings were produced by some superior wisdom and virtue of our own. Intoxicated with unbroken success, we have become too self-sufficient to feel the necessity of redeeming and preserving grace, too proud to pray to the God that made us.[5]

The problems of our culture, from Wall Street to Main Street, and from the White House to the house of God, are beyond any social repair. We do not stand merely in need of better laws, but of better lives, hearts that turn from sin and seek the Lord's will for ourselves and for our country.

Investment: I Will Pay the Price

We are called to live holy lives (Romans 12:1–2), to be salt and light in the midst of a dark world (Matthew 5:13–16), and to call others to repent and believe in the Lord Jesus Christ (Acts 2:38). Moody Church senior pastor Erwin Lutzer encourages the church by declaring:

We are to represent Christ even when the society at large does not. This is not the first time the church has had the responsibility of representing Christ when society as a whole has abandoned God. Indeed, all the churches of the New Testament were islands of righteousness in a sea of paganism. We must recapture the church as an institution for renewal rather than simply an agent for bitter confrontation. We have a hope that transcends the political landscape.[6]

Where may we find the true solution to our national problems? The sixteenth president, Abraham Lincoln, wisely wrote:

> It behooves us, … to humble ourselves before the offended Power, to confess our national sins, to pray for clemency and forgiveness.
>
> Intelligence, Patriotism, Christianity, and a firm reliance on Him who has never yet forsaken this favored land, are still competent to adjust in the best way all our present difficulty.[7]

Convictions: I Will Practice Biblical Principles

We may not always agree with the governing leaders we have, but Scripture offers several ways Christians of all backgrounds and political affiliations can practice biblical principles. First, all Christians are called to pray for their nation and its leaders. Republicans, Democrats, and Independents who claim the name of Jesus are called to come together on the issue of prayer. Paul wrote in 1 Timothy 2:1–4:

> I urge, then, first of all, that petitions, prayers, intercession and thanksgiving be made for all people—for kings and all those in authority, that we may live peaceful and quiet lives in all godliness and holiness. This is good, and pleases God our Savior, who wants all people to be saved and to come to a knowledge of the truth.

Praying for our governing leaders is also a powerful and effective way to see God work in our society. James 5:16 reminds us that "the prayer of a righteous person is powerful and effective." The Great Awakenings of America's past did not begin at the ballot box, but through the divine intervention of the Lord through the prayers of godly men and women. If we long to see America stand strong once again, we need to ask for God's will to be done on earth as it is in heaven (Matthew 5:3).

> Do you know what the candidates believe? Check out state and national candidates at christianvoterguide.com.

Second, Christians can participate by using their right to vote. Those living in the time of Jesus and the apostles did not enjoy the freedom of representative government that we have today. When the prophet Jeremiah wrote to the Jewish exiles in Babylon, he encouraged them to "seek the peace and prosperity of the city to which I have carried you into exile. Pray to the LORD for it, because if it prospers, you too will prosper" (Jeremiah 29:7). They were to seek the good of the nation in which they lived, even when ungodly leaders controlled it.

> Do you vote? This simple question is not as simple as one might think. Many Americans do not take the basic step to vote for who leads their community or country. If you're not registered, then start there. If you are registered to vote, then remember to make time to vote on election day or to vote early if necessary.

Still today, there is a principle that applies beyond prayer. Seeking the peace and prosperity of our communities and nation includes involvement. We are to help select and pursue God-honoring leaders through using our voice to vote, which also includes investigating what candidates believe *and* practice regarding key biblical issues in order to select those leaders who will best lead our land.

Do you know your elected officials? Could you name your governor, congressman or congresswoman, and senators? What about your mayor? Many Americans are far too uninformed regarding their officials. It's hard to pray for people whom you don't know. It's also wise to discover voting records and the stated values of those running for office or for re-election. To find your elected officials, you can log on to usa.gov/elected-officials.

Third, Christians can encourage others to vote according to Christian values. Many Christians do not take this freedom seriously enough. The words of Luke 12:48 could apply to voting, as they teach, "From everyone who has been given much, much will be demanded; and from the one who has been entrusted with much, much more will be asked." As many as 80 million American voters consider themselves Christians.[8] The relatively close 2012 presidential election was won by only about 5 million votes, 65 million votes to 60 million votes. The math clearly shows that if America's Christians mobilized to vote their beliefs, enough voters exist to nominate and choose leaders who stand for God-honoring values, regardless of their political party. If you're registered to vote, vote during every election in your community and encourage others to do the same.

Are you registered to vote? You can't vote your values if you're not registered. Find out how to register at registertovote.org.

Fourth, Christians can join in community transformation. In the early years of our nation, hospitals, universities, schools, children's outreaches, job development, and other areas of community improvement were started and led by followers of Jesus. Yet today some Christians look down on those involved in activism and community development as somehow compromising their faith under the guise of social justice. This does not need to be the case. Godly people can and should continue to serve at the forefront of our nation's most important issues, whether that is fighting poverty, helping those in prison, standing for the lives of unborn children, or assisting women escaping domestic violence.

> What are the organizations working to improve your community? Your church and several agencies are likely already involved. Ask around, find a way to serve, or start your own outreach. It doesn't have to be political; it just needs to help your community.

James 1:27 encourages us, "Religion that God our Father accepts as pure and faultless is this: to look after orphans and widows in their distress and to keep oneself from being polluted by the world." And in Matthew 25:40 Jesus teaches, "Truly I tell you, whatever you did for one of the least of these brothers and sisters of mine, you did for me." Our service to those in need is ultimately service to Christ.

Fifth, more Christians should consider serving in public office. While not every believer in Christ has the abilities or calling to serve in the government, some do. What would happen if every Christian chose to *stop* serving in government? Which policies would be supported? What choices would be made? What level of morality would be seen? Now consider another option: What would happen if every Christian prayed and considered the possibility of serving God through a vocation in government? Numerous additional believers could participate in the positive changes that our society needs at the governmental level. This is the "significant Christian influence" the Bible suggests should be the goal of God's people.

Should *you* run for office? Not many people will run for president, but there are thousands of opportunities to serve at local and state levels in our nation. What would happen if you and other Christians got involved in government? Discover what options are available in your state and community. One good resource to visit is nextinoffice.org /candidate-resources#sos.

Did you know that Congress used to begin with prayer? On September 7, 1774, Jacob Duché prayed:

O LORD, OUR HEAVENLY FATHER, high and mighty King of Kings, and Lord of Lords, who dost from Thy throne behold all the dwellers on earth, and reignest with power supreme and uncontrolled over all the kingdoms, empires and governments; look down in mercy we beseech Thee, on these American States, who have fled to Thee from the rod of the oppressor, and thrown themselves on Thy gracious protection, desiring henceforth to be dependent only on Thee; to Thee they have appealed for the righteousness of their cause; to Thee do they now look up for that countenance and support which Thou alone canst give; take them, therefore, Heavenly Father, under Thy nurturing care; give them wisdom in council and valor in the field; defeat the malicious design of our cruel adversaries; convince them of the unrighteousness of their cause; and if they persist in their sanguinary purpose, O let the voice of Thy own unerring justice, sounding in their hearts, constrain them to drop the weapons of war from their unnerved hands in the day of battle! Be Thou present, O God of wisdom, and direct the counsels of this honorable assembly; enable them to settle things on the best and surest foundation, that the scene of blood may be speedily closed, that order, harmony and peace may be effectually restored, and truth and justice, religion and piety prevail and flourish among Thy people. Preserve the health of their bodies and vigor of their minds; shower down on them, and the millions they here represent, such temporal blessings as Thou seest expedient for them in this world, and crown them with everlasting glory in the world to come. All this we ask in the name and through the merits of Jesus Christ, Thy Son, Our Savior. Amen.[9]

Duché's opening petition could serve as the heart's cry of a new generation of men and women who seek to please the Lord through how we serve and lead the United States.

Will You Stand Strong for America?

It is our desire to encourage you with three reasons why you should and can stand strong for America. These three realities mark our work and we hope will challenge you as we all seek to improve our nation's greatness in the days ahead.

It's Personal

Changing our nation is fundamentally not about who is in the White House, but what happens in your house and in your heart. Are *you* living a life that honors the Lord? True national renewal takes places only when a movement of men and women choose to evaluate their heart and choose to walk according to the ways of God.

What does it mean to follow the Lord? The Great Commandment offers a simple summary: "'Love the Lord your God with all your heart and with all your soul and with all your mind.' This is the first and greatest commandment. And the second is like it: 'Love your neighbor as yourself.' All the Law and the Prophets hang on these two commandments" (Matthew 22:37–40).

When we call out to the Lord for salvation (John 3:16; Romans 10:9), we experience forgiveness and eternal life. With God as our Lord, we seek to live each day in ways that honor Him and help others grow in faith.

ARE YOU A CHURCH LEADER? MOBILIZING YOUR CONGREGATION TO VOTE

According to Project 75, of the 90 million Christians in America, only 39 million are registered to vote. Of those, even fewer actually participate in elections. How can we encourage godly American leadership in government if we do not participate in voting?

Let us encourage you as a church leader to consider three action points for your congregation regarding elections:

1. Personally register to vote and participate in elections.
2. Encourage your congregation's members to register and vote.
3. Equip your congregation regarding important issues related to Christianity and government.

It's Urgent

The Bible speaks about urgency in a number of ways. Our personal salvation is urgent because we are uncertain of how long we will live. Furthermore, Christ will return at any moment, meaning we are to live holy lives each day (1 Thessalonians 4:13–18). Yet the need to stand strong for America is also urgent. Each day that we do not stand strong, events transpire that lead our nation steps closer to a culture in which evil reigns and darkness grows.

Ask any American who has lived through World War II, the Korean War, the Vietnam War, the Cold War, or now lives during our ongoing war against jihadist Islam—do you feel like we have time to spare before we should get serious about living for God and living out His values in our society? When would be a better time to do that? The next generation, the next year, or even the next month? No! There is a growing alarm that America's days of greatness are numbered. The time to stand strong for America is not *someday*; it's right now, today.

While many fear America has already fallen beyond repair, we believe God is not done with our nation yet. Yes, we face difficult circumstances that are ahead, but nothing that God cannot change. As Scripture notes, "If God is for us, who can be against us?" (Romans 8:31). If we live for the Lord and apply His principles to our lives and situations today, who knows how God might work to change our land in the future?

It's Essential

As a speaker, I (Alex) spend a lot of time traveling on airplanes. When I pack, I face two choices: Do I pack whatever I feel like taking, or do I take what is essential? I'll admit, before airlines charged extra for each piece of luggage, I·packed a lot more than I currently do. I wasn't as concerned about a few extra items. Why not? Because it didn't cost me anything. But now that it actually costs me more money to take more stuff, I'm a lot more selective in what I actually pack.

A similar situation exists when we speak about the future of our nation. In the past, perhaps you felt like your role didn't matter as much. You weren't too concerned about getting involved because there were others to help or the situation didn't seem that bad. Even if this might have been true in the past, it is no longer the case today. Your involvement is no longer optional; your commitment is essential.

Any action you take today could change the lives of your immediate family, your community, or even your nation. You'll never know if you don't take the opportunity to stand strong for America where you stand today. As you do, as we do, and as others join us, we'll create a force greater than any political party, as the family of God in America unites to live as "one nation under God, indivisible and with justice for all."

CHAPTER 13

TAKE A STAND

For in your faith you are standing firm.
—2 CORINTHIANS 1:24 NASB

S tanding is a posture that embodies many things. We stand to be seen, we stand to show respect, and we stand up after we fall. Standing is indeed a powerful posture. And that is why Paul encouraged the Christians in his day to "stand firm in the faith" (1 Corinthians 16:13).

Notice that Paul didn't charge Christians to sit down or lie down in their faith, for that would imply an inactive or weak faith. Christians are not called to sit back and do nothing at all; rather, we are commanded by God to stand. To stand for truth and to stand for what is right. To stand and make a difference. People who stand up are those who stand for something. They are passionate pursuers to change lives that will ultimately change the world.

Paul's message back then still applies to us today. Are you standing for Christ? Or are you just sitting around doing nothing? We live in a time when so many Christians say they are followers of Jesus, and yet these same Christians find it difficult to stand up for Christ. The Christian life is a battle. We are at war over so many things: Satan, our sinful desires, and a fallen world that opposes itself against God.

Therefore, as we seek to live out our faith, we are to always be prepared for whatever battle comes our way. Or to put it succinctly, we are to stand strong. Paul writes, "Put on the full armor of God, so that you will be able to stand strong against the schemes of the devil" (Ephesians 6:11 ESV). Elsewhere, Peter tells the persecuted Christians in his day to resist the devil and to be "firm in [their] faith, knowing that the same experiences of suffering are being accomplished by [their] brethren who are in the world" (1 Peter 5:9 NASB).

You see, no matter what you are facing right now, God will give you the strength to stand in the midst of it. It's not a crippled stand, but a stand that says, "I got this because God has me." Let's not kid ourselves—there are times we feel like giving up. But no matter how many times we feel like giving up, God never gives up on each one of us. No matter if you feel lonely, abandoned, frustrated, doubtful, or even hurt, God will give you the strength needed to stand in the raging storm. Things will get tough—sometimes extremely tough—but despite the trial, doubt, turmoil, or fear, there is nothing in this world that can separate you from the love of God.

God is your fortress, and it is God who is your defense. He is the Rock that you can stand on. And so whatever the challenges you face today, if your faith is rooted strongly in the Lord, then you will persist. You will keep on standing. So today—and every day for that matter—turn to the Lord for strength. Pray and ask the Holy Spirit to fill you as you apply the truths found in the Word of God. Take a stand and America will become strong once again.

Reclaiming the Helm of Societal Change

"The church had better stick to preaching the gospel and leave politics alone. That's just all there is to it!" With that declaration, and cocking her head as if to emphasize her point, the woman speaking to me (Alex) turned and quickly walked away. I had just finished speaking in a church's morning service. While shaking hands with people in the lobby afterward, I listened and watched for their feedback. This particular individual was not, I could tell, pleased with what I had presented from the podium.

When I speak on issues that relate to politics and culture, I can be sure that some members of the audience will disapprove no matter what I say. Ingrained in the minds of some Christians is a conviction that the church is not to speak about issues with moral or political overtones. "After all," they suggest, "Christians do not belong to this world, but in the next." The implication is that believers are to keep themselves separate from this world, which is ever-changing, hyperpoliticized, and, according to 2 Peter 3:10, all going to burn up eventually.

It *sounds* so benign and biblical: just love Jesus, assume that your Christian life will somehow make a subtle impression on those around you, and keep your heart from becoming too enamored with this world. But silence (or mixed messages) on the part of many Christians and leaders has resulted in several generations who are now spiritually and morally confused. America has become what our founders warned against—a polarized people divided over numerous issues. Benjamin Franklin warned of the dangers of a divided nation fragmenting itself into divided factions. And yet that's exactly what we are.

Although our culture—and legislators—now grapple with issues about faith, ethics, religious freedom, and the rights of Christian groups, many believers insist that public stances about volatile issues like abortion or gay marriage are not within the scope of the church's mission. Our sole calling, some would suggest, is to *only* proclaim the gospel worldwide and make disciples of every nation (Mark 16:15; Matthew 28:18–20).

But because Scripture does touch on such issues—often in explicit, unmistakable terms—the church of the twenty-first century *must* acknowledge that the Bible has spoken. We must share with others what the Word of God has said. About the "tough issues," let's be honest: a biblically informed position *can* be determined. The problem for many Christians is not that a biblically informed stance is unknowable, but that it is unpopular. To stand up for Christian truth these days takes courage. Urgently needed is a generation of Christians who model conviction, maturity, discernment, and involvement. Remember that we are called to be salt and light in the world, which, by definition, requires active involvement in the world.

Holding the Church Accountable

In key areas of cultural leadership, persons with solidly held Christian convictions once wielded significant influence. It was expected that Christians take public stands on key issues, and God's people actually exerted tangible cultural influence. Christians were the leaders in society, making a difference in many different areas, including science, the fine arts, literature, education, and politics.

Many contemporary Christian thinkers believe that the societal ills of today can be traced to nearly a century of the Western church's failure to teach and defend the biblical worldview. And past cultural leaders—Francis Schaeffer (philosopher), Charles Colson (political thinker), Jerry Falwell (leader in education), C. S. Lewis (scholar and novelist), Mother Teresa (fighter of poverty), Cardinal Avery Dulles (theologian), and Richard John Neuhaus (defender of life), to name but a few—would certainly concur.

All of these past leaders recognized that the church in every age is a mixture of things current and things ancient, the popular and the timeless. There is a need for, and, indeed, an inevitability of, the church to interact with the present world. The church must give every generation God's "take" on things, both social and political. It may not be the assignment that we pilgrims would request for ourselves, but no matter the case, it is the assignment we are given.

The Church Is the Conscience of the Culture[1]

At a time when so many reject the concept of absolute truth, and multitudes more often embrace a do-it-yourself spirituality, what may the church do? How should we proceed? Remember that the church in every generation is commissioned with the responsibility to pass the faith on to the next generation. What ultimately happens when churches do not effectively pass the baton of faith continues to be evident. Research by the National Study of Youth and Religion recently showed:

> Most American teens have a creed that is far from Christianity, with no place for sin, judgment, salvation, or Christ. [They] believe in a combination of works righteousness, religion as psychological well-being, and a distant non-interfering god.[2]

It is time that people experience anew the God who has intervened in history, and whose kingdom will one day cover the earth "as the waters cover the sea" (Habakkuk 2:14). The people who know this God are commissioned to help point the way for those who do not. A way to initiate the process is to respectfully talk with people about what God's Word has to say regarding controversial issues—even the ones in which the biblical position is unpopular.

A ROAD MAP TO RESTORING AMERICA

Live the Gospel

The order of any Christian is to live a life worthy of the gospel of Jesus Christ (Philippians 1:27). The great C. H. Spurgeon once said, "If you do not die to sin, you shall die for sin."[1] Christians are not to pursue the desires of the flesh (1 Peter 1:14), nor are they to love the things in the world (1 John 2:15). Therefore, as citizens of heaven (Philippians 3:20), live every day for Christ, and not for yourself. Be Christ to others, and see the difference it will make in your life, as well as in the lives of others.

Proclaim the Gospel

We are to tell the whole world about Jesus Christ. That is not an option; it's a command. Jesus said, "Go into all the world and preach the gospel to all creation" (Mark 16:15). The world would radically change for the better if every single Christian boldly shared the gospel with his or her unsaved family members, neighbors, and friends. If you want to impact your nation for the better, then be proactive in sharing the gospel with others.

Build Stronger Families

The most powerful institution and outlet of God's grace and love is the family. Make it your aim every day to build up your family, rather than tearing it down. One way to restore families is by setting a good example in your own family. A strong family can go a long way in the midst of all the broken ones (Psalm 127:1; Ephesians 5:22–33; 6:4). Keep loving and forgiving your spouse and training your children in the Word of God.

Be a Mentor

Mentors are few and far between, because most people don't see themselves as one. Much of the vacancy in leadership is due to a lack of true mentors. There comes a time in your Christian walk that you need to say, as Paul did, "Imitate me, just as I also imitate Christ" (1 Corinthians 11:1 NKJV). Hard to say. Hard to live. But this country needs more mentors. So if you are a mentor, may the Lord take your ministry to new heights. But if you are not a mentor yet, find a mentor who can pour into you and help you impact the lives of others in return.

Give and Serve

A significant life is one of giving and serving. Jesus didn't come to be served, but to serve (Matthew 20:28). He served to the point that He gave up His life so that we can have eternal life. The more you give of yourself, even if it's inconvenient, the greater the reward. Take some time and evaluate how much you are giving and serving. Make some adjustments so that you can maximize your life to give and serve even more. And consider these words from the apostle Paul: "Whatever you do, work heartily, as for the Lord and not for men, knowing that from the Lord you will receive the inheritance as your reward. You are serving the Lord Christ" (Colossians 3:23–24 ESV).

Vote Biblically

What would you do if you received an e-mail that indicated your neighborhood had the chance of receiving free yard care, home pest control treatment, around-the-clock security, and free car washes for an entire year? All you had to do was show up to vote for it. Would you do it? Of course you would. Well, in many ways, that's a lot like political elections. When Christians don't care enough to vote for strong candidates who embody biblical principles, then they are losing out in a big way.

Did you know that more than 75 percent of Christians don't vote? That means Christians aren't taking advantage of one of their greatest privileges as an American citizen. That's pathetic. Thus, make it a top priority to study the most moral and honest candidates, get out to vote, and encourage your family and friends to do the same. You may think your vote doesn't matter, but it does. If only 10 percent more Christians regularly voted in local and statewide elections, they would essentially take almost any election. Could you imagine what would happen in America as a result?

Be a Voice

Every day more than four thousand unborn babies are aborted. Since 1973, nearly 60 million babies' lives have been horrifically ended before they even began. Unborn babies are human beings. They have rights. They have a right to life just like every other human. However, they don't have a voice. No one asks them if they want to live or die. Be a voice for the thousands of unborn babies. Stand up and make a difference by getting involved in the pro-life movement. You can become a sidewalk counselor outside your local abortion clinic, you can pray and give monthly to a pro-life organization, or you can serve as a volunteer and provide care items needed for those mommies who choose life. Don't ignore this atrocity that our country has permitted to take place. Be a voice for life!

Make It Happen

People have good intentions, but the problem is that their intentions often never get off the ground. But those who finish what they started make a difference. So the more Christians get out there and make it happen, the greater influence and impact they will be in their neighborhoods, schools, workplaces, and churches. If God has called you to fulfill some task for His name's sake, then make it happen. Don't give up. If God has called you, He has also enabled you to make it happen.

Learn More

How would you rate your level of knowledge of the Bible? Would you say you are a strong defender of the Christian faith? If some atheist or even a Muslim were to attack your faith, would you be able to adequately respond? Despite all the information at our fingertips, Christians are more biblically illiterate than ever before. To help overcome this illiteracy trend, here are a few tips to get Christians to learn all the more. First, take anywhere from twenty to thirty minutes a day to pray, read the Bible, and read other books that will sharpen your knowledge about Christianity. Second, get with a few close friends and go through a Christian book together. Third, get engaged with our television and radio ministry, *Viral Truth*. You can check it out at viraltruth.com.

Always Be Grateful

It's easy to be a grump and complain. But the Bible reminds us to "give thanks in all circumstances; for this is the will of God in Christ Jesus for you" (1 Thessalonians 5:18 ESV). A heart of gratitude can go a long way. Christians who demonstrate a grateful heart are the most warm and contagious kinds of people in the world. Be sensitive as to how you treat others, and always give thanks to God for your many and constant blessings.

APPENDIX 2

ORGANIZATIONS TO SUPPORT

Family Research Council

frc.org

Family Research Council's vision is a culture in which human life is valued, families flourish, and religious liberty thrives. Family Research Council's mission is to advance faith, family, and freedom in public policy and the culture from a Christian worldview.

American Family Association

afa.net

The mission of the American Family Association is to inform, equip, and activate individuals to strengthen the moral foundations of American culture, and give aid to the church here and abroad in its task of fulfilling the Great Commission.

The American Family Association believes that God has communicated absolute truth to mankind, and that all people are subject to the authority of God's Word at all times. Therefore, AFA believes that a culture based on biblical truth best serves the well-being of our nation and our families, in accordance with the vision of our founding documents; and that personal transformation through the Gospel of Jesus Christ is the greatest agent of biblical change in any culture.

Alliance Defending Freedom

adflegal.org

Alliance Defending Freedom advocates for your right to freely live out your faith.

The Heritage Foundation

heritage.org

Founded in 1973, The Heritage Foundation is a research and educational institution—a think tank—whose mission is to formulate and promote conservative public policies based on the principles of free enterprise, limited government, individual freedom, traditional American values, and a strong national defense.

The Heritage Foundation believes the principles and ideas of the American founding are worth conserving and renewing. As policy entrepreneurs, they believe the most effective solutions are consistent with those ideas and principles. Their vision is to build an America where freedom, opportunity, prosperity, and civil society flourish.

Family Policy Alliance

familypolicyalliance.com

The vision of Family Policy Alliance is a nation where God is honored, religious freedom flourishes, families thrive and life is cherished. Their mission is to advance biblical citizenship, equip statesmen, promote policy and serve an effective alliance, all committed to a common vision.

Christian Coalition of America

cc.org

Christian Coalition offers people of faith the vehicle to be actively involved in impacting the issues they care about—from the county courthouse to the halls of Congress.

The Coalition is a political organization, made up of pro-family Americans who care deeply about ensuring that government serves to strengthen and preserve, rather than threaten, our families and our values. To that end, they work continuously to identify, educate and mobilize Christians for effective political action.

The Stand Strong Tour

standstrongtour.com

The Stand Strong Tour unites thousands of Christians, young and old, and in churches all across America, to become equipped with a biblical worldview. Each tour has six worldview weekend series designed to specifically teach and equip Christians, whether that is surrounding their marriage and family, their work, life in college, or addressing religious freedoms in America today.

Each Stand Strong worldview series is designed to help Christians stand strong by becoming emboldened in their faith, equipped with a biblical worldview, and engaged in winning their sphere of influence for Christ.

Stand Strong Ministries

standstrongministries.org

Our vision is to reinforce Christians to stand strong no matter the cost. Our mission is to help Christians move from uninformed, confused, and disengaged—to grounded disciples of Christ with a solid biblical worldview. Our training is fulfilled with our e3 strategy: embolden, equip, and engage.

READER'S DISCUSSION GUIDE

Chapter 1 – How Christianity Shaped America's Foundation

1. Should the founders' many references to God, morality, and Christianity still be seen as relevant for today? What bearing should their spiritual beliefs have on us in the twenty-first century?

2. It is commonly assumed that America's founders were secularists who were probably motivated more by political and economic opportunity than by any type of "sacred" calling. In light of this, how would George Washington's two-hour prayer meeting be received today? Could a US president ever again be so overt about his or her faith?

3. Have you looked into what your state's charter and constitution have to say about God? Become familiar with this content and share it with others as a way to begin a conversation about the direction our nation is heading.

4. If America's true heritage is forgotten, or if it is intentionally revised and distorted, what will be the end result? To what degree should each citizen feel an obligation to know the facts of history and to share such knowledge with others?

Chapter 2 – Dreams of Our Fathers

1. What are some things that are different about America now than how America was in the past?

2. What do you suppose the founders would say if they saw what America has become today? Do you think they would approve or disapprove of the changes?
3. In what ways has your faith impacted your life?
4. Do you agree with the authors when they suggest that America has lost community? Why or why not?
5. What are some ways Americans can rebuild community in their lives?

Chapter 3 - God and Country: A True Story

1. Which of America's original governmental documents mandates "the separation of church and state"?
2. What was Thomas Jefferson's original intent for the First Amendment?
3. Who wrote the First Amendment in its current form? What was his spiritual orientation?
4. Can you cite a US Supreme Court decision that addresses the role of religion in American life? What has been the consensus of our nation's highest court on this issue?
5. How do you think Thomas Jefferson would react to the ways in which acknowledgments of God, morality, the Bible, Christianity, and religious freedom are suppressed today?

Chapter 4 - Uncommon Common Sense

1. The colonists didn't stand a chance against England, and yet they won the American Revolution. How do you suppose they did it?
2. What contributions did Alexander Hamilton, James Madison, and Thomas Jefferson have in shaping the United States of America?

3. Why is the Constitution of the United States so important to America, and why should Americans care about
   it today?
4. What is natural law and why did our founders think it
   was so important?
5. Why is the belief in God so fundamental to the existence of the United States of America?

Chapter 5 – America: Freedom *of* Religion, not Freedom *from* Religion

1. Groups like the Freedom from Religion Foundation
   speak of "the constitutional principle of separation of
   church and state." And yet, as we have documented so
   far, no such wording or principle is contained in the US
   Constitution. Do you think that such groups are aware
   of this? And do you think such "spin" and historical
   revision is proof of a movement to erase God from
   public consciousness?
2. What was America's first governmental document?
   What purposes or intents did it set forth?
3. What percentage of the founders' writings and quotes
   cite the Holy Bible?
4. According to the second US president, John Adams,
   what was the foundation of America? What was the
   prevailing worldview that guided the founders?
5. John Adams spoke of how the Constitution was written for "a moral and religious people," and stated, "It
   is wholly inadequate to the government of any other."
   Why would nonmoral, nonreligious people have a
   problem with the Constitution as written?

Chapter 6 – America Is Dying: Threats from Within

1. What are some governing policies that are destroying America? What are some solutions to putting a stop to those policies?
2. America went from losing her innocence to losing authority, to losing love, to losing hope, to losing reason, to losing her imagination. What do you suppose America will lose next?
3. In what ways has apathy affected your life? Have you been able to overcome it? Why or why not?
4. What are some areas in the Christian faith that you are ignorant of? How do you plan to overcome this ignorance?
5. We see the growing trend of narcissism that is consuming Americans today. Read Philippians 2 and 1 Peter 5, and then write down some ways in which to overcome pride in your life.

Chapter 7 – America Is under Attack: Four Threats from Beyond

1. The Gay Revolution is trying to push its agenda into the forefront of America's culture. In what ways can you be firm in your convictions to the Word of God and yet still demonstrate the love of God to individuals embracing this type of lifestyle? What are some practical ways you can outlast the Gay Revolution?
2. In Jason's conversation with Erick Stakelbeck, Erick said the reason we, as Americans, don't care about ISIS in the Middle East is because of the prosperity we are currently experiencing, as well as how we are so wrapped up in our own lives. How can we as

individuals, and particularly as Christians who live in America, begin to care about what is taking place in the world today?

3. What is the difference between a secularist and a militant secularist?

4. Do you think it is important that the United States of America stands with Israel today? Why or why not?

5. Make a plan on how you can reach homosexuals, Muslims, and atheists with the gospel of Jesus Christ.

Chapter 8 – A Noble Vine: Then and Now

1. What was the stated purpose of the first Thanksgiving celebrations?

2. In his presidential Thanksgiving proclamation, what was George Washington's stated objective for the holiday?

3. What things are you most thankful for about America? Do you think that our heritage, which is steeped in Christianity, makes our citizens more accountable to God? If so, how might our obligations to God be lived out?

4. What would be the reaction by those you know regarding the Christian origin of America's "Ivy League" universities? How might God and facts about Christianity be reintroduced to academia in the US once again?

5. In this chapter we list six approaches to the issue of government's relationship with religion. Which perspective resonates with you the most? Is your view about this compatible with what our nation's founders would have supported?

Chapter 9 – A More Perfect Union

1. What about self-governance makes America so great?

2. What are some of the problems that are being caused by disconnected Americans? Is there any way to reconnect them to reality? If so, then how?
3. What value does America bring to the rest of the world? Do you think it's important that America remains the greatest nation on earth? Why or why not?
4. Are you hopeful about the future? Why or why not?
5. In what areas of your life do you need to refocus your priorities?
6. Who has been a model of courage in your life, and why?

Chapter 10: The Courts and Christianity

1. What did Abraham Lincoln say was the only safeguard of our liberties?
2. The New England states were largely settled by Puritans in the mid to late seventeenth century. Think about how their Christian values, work ethic, and morality shaped this first wave of American culture.
3. Citing Matthew 5:14, what did Puritan John Winthrop call this new nation? Winthrop spoke of a "covenant" and a divine "commission"—do you think these concepts still apply today?
4. In what ways is the Puritan view of life's purpose (and good citizenship) different from the priorities that drive people today?

Chapter 11 - Wake up, Church

1. How are you praying for your pastors and your church?
2. Why is being politically correct not so correct?
3. What are your spiritual gifts and how are you using them to further expand the kingdom of God?

4. In this chapter we talked about egocentric churches versus Christ-centered churches. What's the difference between the two and how can you help more people get connected with a Bible-teaching church?

5. Make a list of churches in your area. Devote a whole month to pray and intercede for each one of them. At the end of the month, send a note or an e-mail to let them know how you prayed for them.

Chapter 12 – Your Role in Restoring America's True Greatness

1. Ten things are listed as examples of our modern abandonment of God. Do you think that such realities constitute "national sin"? Which of them are the most serious?

2. Some people scoff at the idea of a "Christian nation," or, in business, at the idea of a "Christian company." What might be a distinction between a "Christian" and a "Christian country"? How may we defend the idea of a Christian nation?

3. For decades Christianity had "home court advantage" in America and the West. In media, education, politics, and in the culture at large, morality and godly principles were overwhelmingly influential. In what ways do twenty-first-century Christians have to adjust to life as a marginalized group?

4. If the Christian's true home is heaven, then why should we care about politics and what happens during our lifetimes?

5. Should a Christian register and vote? And should believers persuade others to do so?

Chapter 13 – Take a Stand

1. What are some things you could personally begin to do this week that would contribute to the much-needed restoration of America? How about over the next thirty days? Six months? Or even how about over the next one to three years?

2. It may sound ambitious, but you can be used by God to change the world. Do you truly believe this? What action would you attempt for Christ if you knew that He would bless and use it?

3. What would you strive to accomplish in this life if you knew that leaving it undone would result in some great loss?

4. Please read 1 Corinthians 15:58. What is Paul's admonition to the people of Corinth and thus to us in our own day?

ENDNOTES

Introduction

1. George Washington, quoted in Isaac Backus, *A History of New England with Particular Reference to the Denomination Called Baptists*, vol. 2 (Newton, MA: The Backus Historical Society, 1871), 340.
2. "A Conversation with Robert Frost," interview by Bela Kornizer, *NBC News*, November 23, 1952, NBC Learn K-12, https://archives.nbclearn.com/portal/site/k-12/browse/?cuecard=62594.
3. Charles F. Adams, *Letters of John Adams: Addressed to His Wife* (Boston: Freeman and Bolles, 1841), 218.

Chapter 1: How Christianity Shaped America's Foundation

1. George Washington, "The First Thanksgiving Proclamation," October 3, 1789, as cited in Timothy L. Hall, *Religion in America* (New York: InfoBase Publishing, 2007), 369.
2. James Madison, quoted in Mark Sutherland, *Judicial Tyranny: The New Kings of America* (St. Louis: Amerisearch, Inc., 2005), 56.
3. Alexis de Tocqueville, *Democracy in America* (New York: Harper and Rowe, 1966), 303–304.
4. Christopher Columbus, *Book of Prophecies*, as found in Washington Irving, *Life and Voyages of Christopher Columbus*, (New York, NY: The Cooperative Publication Society, Inc., 1892), 41. See also Gary de Mar, *God and Government*, vol. 1 (Atlanta, GA: American Press, 1982), 126.
5. Christopher Columbus and Andres Bernaldez, *The Voyages of Christopher Columbus*, trans. and ed. Jane Cecil (London: Argonaut Press, 1930), 146.
6. Washington, "Thanksgiving Proclamation."
7. Quoted in James D. Kennedy, *What If Jesus Had Never Been Born?* (Nashville, TN: Thomas Nelson, 1994), 164–65.
8. Sir William Berkley, "Charter of Carolina," March 24, 1663, Lillian Goldman Law Library, http://avalon.law.yale.edu/17th_century/nc01.asp.

9. "The Fundamental Constitutions of the Carolinas," March 1, 1669, Lillian Goldman Law Library, http:// http://avalon.law.yale.edu/17th_century/nc05.asp.

10. "Constitution of North Carolina," December 18, 1776, Lillian Goldman Law Library, http://avalon.law.yale.edu/18th_century/nc07.asp, article XXXII. It is important to note that in 1835 the word *Protestant* was changed to the word *Christian*.

11. Adapted from Alex McFarland, "Strip This Away and America Is Doomed," *Charisma News*, July 21, 2014, http://www.charismanews.com/opinion/44723-strip-this-away-and-america-is-absolutely-doomed.

Chapter 2: Dreams of Our Fathers

1. John Winthrop, *A Model of Christian Charity* (1630), quoted in Suzanne McIntire, *Speeches in World History* (New York: Infobase Publishing, 2009), 143.

2. Ibid.

3. Henry Drummond, *The Ideal Life: Listening for God's Voice, Discerning His Leading* (New Kensington, PA: Whitaker House Publishing, 2014), chapter 6.

Chapter 3: God and Country: A True Story

1. George Santayana, *The Life of Reason: Reason in Common Sense* (New York: Scribner's, 1905), 284.

2. Neil Cogan, ed., *The Complete Bill of Rights: Proposed by Madison* (Oxford: Oxford University Press, 2015), 1.

3. Roger Williams, "Mr. Cotton's Letter Lately Printed, Examined and Answered," *The Complete Writings of Roger Williams* (New York: Russell & Russell Inc. 1963), vol. 1, 108, quoted in Bruce T. Gourley, project developer, "Quotes," Church/State Separation: A Historical Primer, http://www.wallof-separation.us/quotes/.

4. Congressional Record, 149:15, July 28, 2003 to September 5, 2003.

5. Thomas Jefferson, "To Moses Robinson Washington," March 23, 1801, American History from Revolution to Reconstruction and beyond, http://www.let.rug.nl/usa/presidents/thomas-jefferson/letters-of-thomas-jefferson/jefl138.php.

6. Henry P. Johnston, ed., *The Correspondence and Public Papers of John Jay*, vol. IV (New York: Burt Franklin, 1970), 393.

7. Joseph Story, quoted in Robert Cord, *Separation of Church and State: Historical Fact and Current Fiction* (New York: Lambeth Press, 1982), 13.

8. Everson v. Board of Education of the Township of Ewing, N.J., 52, 330 U.S. 1 (1947).

9. Chief Justice Warren Burger, "Excerpts from Supreme Court's Opinion and Dissent on Municipal Creche," *New York Times*, March 6, 1984, http://www.nytimes.com/1984/03/06/us/excerpts-from-supreme-court-s-opinion-and-dissent-on-municipal-creche.html.

10. Franklin D. Roosevelt, "Address to the Nation," December 24, 1944, The American Presidency Project, http://www.presidency.ucsb.edu/ws/?pid=16485.

11. Thomas Jefferson, "Virginia Act for Establishing Religious Freedom," January 16, 1786, The Heritage Foundation, http://www.heritage.org/initiatives/first-principles/primary-sources/virginia-act-establishing-religious-freedom.

12. Abraham Lincoln, quoted in Robert Flood, *The Rebirth of America* (St. Davids, PA: The Arthur S. DeMoss Foundation, 1986), 32.

Chapter 4: Uncommon Common Sense

1. Thomas Paine, *Common Sense* (Philadelphia: W. and T. Bradford, 1776), quoted at Bartleby.com, http://www.bartleby.com/133/.

2. Thomas Jefferson, *The Writings of Thomas Jefferson* (1854), quoted in Joyce Appleby, ed., and Terrence Ball, *Political Writings by Thomas Jefferson* (Cambridge: University Press, 2005), 613.

3. George Washington, quoted in John Fea, *Was America Founded as a Christian Nation?: A Historical Introduction* (Louisville, KY: Westminster John Knox, 2011), 188.

4. James Madison, address to the General Assembly of the State of Virginia, 1778.

5. Jason Jimenez, *The Raging War of Ideas* (Maitland, FL: Xulon Press, 2012), 178.

Chapter 5: America: Freedom of Religion, not Freedom from Religion

1. Jonah Hicap, "Louisiana educates rights group: 'Freedom of religion, not freedom from religion,'" *Christianity Today*, http://www.christiantoday.com/article/louisiana.educates.atheists.its.freedom.of.religion.not.freedom.from.religion/66523.htm.

2. The Freedom from Religion Foundation, http://ffrf.org.

3. George Washington, "Letter to the United Baptist Churches of Virginia," May 10, 1789, quoted at *Beliefnet*, http://www.beliefnet.com/resourcelib/docs/91/Letter_from_George_Washington_to_the_United_Baptist_Churches__1.html.

4. "About the First Amendment," The First Amendment Center, http://www.firstamendmentcenter.org/about-the-first-amendment.

5. Ronald Reagan, "Remarks at an Ecumenical Prayer Breakfast in Dallas, Texas August 23, 1984," *The Public Papers of President Ronald W. Reagan,* Ronald Reagan Presidential Library, https://reaganlibrary.archives.gov /archives/speeches/1984/82384a.htm.

6. George Washington, quoted in William Jackson Johnstone, *George Washington the Christian* (New York: Abingdon, 1919), 24–35.

7. Ibid., 24.

8. Benjamin Franklin, quoted in "Religion and the Founding of the American Republic," Library of Congress, http://www.loc.gov/exhibits/religion/rel06 .html.

9. Benjamin Franklin, quoted in Richard Saunders, *Poor Richards Improved Almanac* (May 31, 1757; Waterloo, IA: U.S.C. Publishing, 1914).

10. William Federer, *America's God and Country: Encyclopedia of Quotations* (St. Louis: Amerisearch, Inc., 2000).

11. Patrick Henry, quoted in William J. Federer, *Change to Chains: 6000 Year Quest for Control,* vol. I, *Rise of the Republic* (St. Louis: Amerisearch, 2011), 250.

12. John Adams and Charles Francis Adams, *The Works of John Adams: Second President of the United States,* vol. 10 (Boston: Little, Brown, and Company, 1856), 43.

13. John Adams, message to the officers of the First Brigade of the Third Division of the Militia of Massachusetts, October 11, 1798.

14. Thomas Jefferson, "Proclamation Appointing a Day of Thanksgiving and Prayer, 11 November 1779," Founders Online, National Archives, http:// founders.archives.gov/documents/Jefferson/01-03-02-0187. Source: *The Papers of Thomas Jefferson,* vol. 3, *18 June 1779–30 September 1780,* ed. Julian P. Boyd (Princeton: Princeton University Press, 1951), 177–79.

15. Thomas Jefferson, *Notes on the State of Virginia,* Query XVIII, quoted in "Notes on the State of Virginia," *Wikipedia,* https://en.wikipedia.org/w /index.php?title=Notes_on_the_State_of_Virginia&oldid=710096381.

16. Mark A. Bellies and Jerry Newcombe, *Doubting Thomas? The Religious Life and Legacy of Thomas Jefferson* (New York: Morgan James Publishing, 2015).

17. "From Thomas Jefferson to Moses Robinson, 23 March 1801," Founders Online, National Archives, http://founders.archives.gov/documents /Jefferson/01-33-02-0362. Source: *The Papers of Thomas Jefferson,* vol. 33, *17 February–30 April 1801,* ed. Barbara B. Oberg (Princeton: Princeton University Press, 2006), 423–24.

18. "From Thomas Jefferson to Peter Carr, with Enclosure, 10 August 1787," Founders Online, National Archives, http://founders.archives.gov /documents/Jefferson/01-12-02-0021. Source: *The Papers of Thomas Jefferson*, vol. 12, *7 August 1787–31 March 1788*, ed. Julian P. Boyd (Princeton: Princeton University Press, 1955), 14–19.

19. Thomas Jefferson, letter dated May 5, 1803, quoted in Mark Beliles, ed., *The Selected Religious Letters and Papers of Thomas Jefferson* (Charlottesville, VA: America Publications, 2013), 114.

20. Samuel Adams, quoted in James D. Kennedy, *What If Jesus Had Never Been Born?* (Nashville, TN: Thomas Nelson, 1994), 67.

21. *Barnard's American Journal of Education* 27 (January 1, 1877): 613.

22. Samuel Adams, letter to John Adams (1790), in *Four Letters: Being an Interesting Correspondence Between Those Eminently Distinguished Characters, John Adams, Late President of the United States; and Samuel Adams, Late Governor of Massachusetts. On the Important Subject of Government* (Boston: Adams and Rhoades, 1802), 9–10.

23. John Quincy Adams, quoted in Federer, *America's God and Country*, 19.

24. John Quincy Adams, quoted in William H. Seward, *Life and Public Services of John Quincy Adams* (New York: C.M. Saxton, Barker & Co., 1860), 248–49.

25. Andrew Johnson, quoted in Federer, *America's God and Country*, 334.

26. Noah Webster, *Webster's American Dictionary of the English Language* (1828), preface.

27. Abraham Lincoln, "Proclamation Appointing a National Fast Day," March 30, 1863, Abraham Lincoln Online, http://www.abrahamlincolnonline.org /lincoln/speeches/fast.htm. Source: *Collected Works of Abraham Lincoln*, ed. Roy P. Basler et al.

28. Grover Cleveland, quoted in William J. Federer, ed., *Prayers and Presidents: Inspiring Faith from Leaders of the Past* (St. Louis: AmeriSearch, 2010), 115.

29. Woodrow Wilson, quoted in Gary Scott Smith, *Faith and Presidency from George Washington to George W. Bush* (New York: Oxford University Press, 2006).

30. Woodrow Wilson, quoted in Federer, *America's God and Country*, 741.

31. Bobby Jindal, quoted in Craig Millward, "Gov. Jindal: 'America Did Not Create Religious Liberty, Religious Liberty Created America,'" CNSNews, http://cnsnews.com/blog/craig-millward/gov-jindal-america-did-not -create-religious-liberty-religious-liberty-created.

32. A. W. Tozer, quoted in Michael Brown, "Who Changed Things?," *Charisma News*, February 17, 2014, http://www.charismanews.com/opinion /in-the-line-of-fire/42808-who-changed-things.

Chapter 6: America Is Dying: Threats from Within

1. "Washington's Farewell Address," September 19, 1796, The Heritage Foundation, http://www.heritage.org/initiatives/first-principles/primary-sources/ washingtons-farewell-address.
2. Mark Levine, *Plunder and Deceit* (New York: Threshold Editions, 2015), 5.
3. David Kupelian, *The Snapping of the American Mind* (Washington, DC: WND Books, 2015), 10.
4. Ravi Zacharias, *Recapture the Wonder* (Nashville, TN: Thomas Nelson, 2005), 42–43.
5. Paul Kengor, *Takedown: From Communists to Progressives, How the Left Has Sabotaged Family and Marriage* (Washington, DC: WND Books, 2015), 12–13.
6. Michelle A. Vu, "George Barna: America Is Being Destroyed Inside Out," *Christian Post*, May 7, 2009, http://www.christianpost.com/news/ george-barna-america-is-being-destroyed-inside-out-38539/.
7. Jim Parsons, "The Cohabitation Formulation," *The Big Bang Theory*, season 4, episode 16, directed by Mark Cendrowski, aired February 17, 2011 on CBS.
8. Maureen Stearns, *Conscious Courage: Turning Everyday Challenges into Opportunities* (Seminole, FL: Enrichment, 2004), 99.
9. Valerie Richardson, "Houston mayor withdraws pastor subpoenas after national uproar," *Washington Times*, October 29, 2014, http://www.washingtontimes.com/news/2014/oct/29/ houston-mayor-withdraws-pastor-subpoenas.
10. John Adams and Charles Francis Adams, *The Works of John Adams, Second President of the United States* (Boston: Little, Brown, 1850), 456.
11. Calvin Coolidge, quoted in Noel Sheppard, "Someone's Dying for Your Vote," *RealClearPolitics*, http://www.realclearpolitics.com/articles/2006/10/ someones_dying_for_your_vote.html.
12. Benjamin Franklin, quoted in John A Roush, "The Expense of Ignorance and the Value of Accountability," *Huffington Post*, updated July 25, 2012, http://www.huffingtonpost.com/john-roush/education-accountability_b_1546520.html.

13. Dr. Keith Ablow, "We are raising a generation of deluded narcissists," January 8, 2013, *Fox News*, http://www.foxnews.com/opinion/2013/01/08/ are-raising-generation-deluded-narcissists.html.
14. Ibid.
15. Dr. John Townsend, *The Entitlement Cure: Finding Success in Doing Hard Things the Right Way* (Grand Rapids, MI: Zondervan, 2015), 22–23.
16. J. M. Twenge and J. D. Foster, "Birth cohort increases in narcissistic personality traits among American college students, 1982–2009," *Social Psychological and Personality Science* 1 (2011), 99–106. See also S. H. Konrath, E. H. O'Brien, and C. Hsing, "Changes in dispositional empathy in American college students over time: A meta-analysis," *Personality and Social Psychology Review,* 15 (2011), 180–98.

Chapter 7: America Is under Attack: Four Threats from Beyond

1. James Dobson, *Family Talk* (Colorado Springs, CO: June 2014). See also Bob Unruh, "James Dobson: Christians Soon to Be 'Hated Minority,'" *WND*, April 22, 2015, http://www.wnd.com/2015/04/ christians-facing-new-status-as-hated-minority/.
2. Kengor, *Takedown*, 2–3.
3. Dobson, *Family Talk*. See also Bob Unruh, "James Dobson: Christians Soon to Be 'Hated Minority,'" *WND*, http://www.wnd.com/2015/04/christians -facing-new-status-as-hated-minority/.
4. Michael Brown, *Outlasting the Gay Revolution* (WND Books, 2015), quoted in John Stonestreet, "Breakpoint This Week: Outlasting the Gay Revolution," BreakPoint, July 3, 2015, http://www.breakpoint.org/features-columns /discourse/entry/15/27739.
5. David Ignatius, "James Clapper: We underestimated the Islamic State's 'will to fight,'" *Washington Post*, September 18, 2014, https:// www.washingtonpost.com/opinions/david-ignatius-we-under- estimated-the-islamic-state-james-clapper-says/2014/09/18/ f0f17072-3f6f-11e4-9587-5dafd96295f0_story.html.
6. Erick Stakelbeck, *ISIS Exposed: Beheadings, Slavery, and the Hellish Reality of Radical Islam* (Washington, DC: Regnery Publishing, 2015), 12.
7. Trey Sanchez, "Now at Vanderbilt: Conservative Professor Targeted by Offended Students," *Truth Revolt*, November 11, 2105, http://www.truthrevolt.org/news/ now-vanderbilt-conservative-professor-targeted-offended-students.

8. William Craig Lane, transcript of Reasonable Faith podcast from April 13, 2014, in which Kevin Harris and Craig discuss *A Manual for Creating Atheists* by Peter Boghossian (Pitchstone Publishing, 2013), http://www.reasonablefaith.org/a-manual-for-creating-atheists#ixzz3rrUKo4A7.

9. John F. Kennedy, quoted in Mitchell Geoffrey Bard, *The Complete Idiot's Guide to the Middle East Conflict* (New York: Penguin Group, 2008), 13.

10. Ronald Reagan, Office of Public Communication, Bureau of Public Affairs, *The Department of State Bulletin*, vol. 84, 1984.

11. Thomas Jefferson, quoted in Bradley Scott, *18 Quotes from American Presidents About Israel, TheBlaze*, April 28, 2014, http://www.theblaze.com/contributions/18-quotes-from-american-presidents-about-israel-2/.

12. George W. Bush, "President's Remarks at National Dinner Celebrating Jewish Life in America" (Washington, DC: Office of the Press Secretary, September 14, 2005), http://georgewbush-whitehouse.archives.gov/news/releases/2005/09/text/20050914-24.html.

13. George Washington, quoted in Steven Coffman, *Words of the Founding Fathers: Selected Quotations of Franklin, Washington, Adams, Jefferson, Madison and Hamilton, with Sources* (Jefferson, NC: McFarland, 2012), 23.

14. Ibid.

Chapter 8: A Noble Vine: Then and Now

1. Jonathan Dickson, quoted in Stephen K. McDowell and Mark A. Beliles, *America's Providential History* (Charlottesville, VA: Providence Press, 1988), 93.

2. Jonathan Edwards, *The Works of Jonathan Edwards*, vol. 1 (Great Britain: Bath Press, 1995), 171.

3. Edward Winslow, quoted in James Deetz and Patricia Scott Deetz, *Times of Their Lives: Life, Love, and Death in Plymouth Colony* (New York: Anchor, 2001).

4. William Bradford, quoted in William Federer, *America's God and Country: Encyclopedia of Quotations* (St. Louis: Amerisearch, Inc., 2000), 66.

5. John Quincy Adams, quoted in Charles F. Adams, *Letters of John Adams: Addressed to His Wife* (Boston: Freeman and Bolles, 1841), 218.

6. According to Daniel Webster, Jefferson said this to him. See Daniel Webster to Professor Pease, June 15, 1852, in Edward Everett, ed., *The Writings and Speeches of Daniel Webster*, (Boston: Little, Brown & Co., 1903), 16:656.

7. Benjamin Rush, "A Defence of the Use of the Bible in Schools," 1791, WallBuilders, http://wallbuilders.com/LIBissuesArticles.asp?id=147036.

8. *New England Primer* (1805).

9. William Lyon Phelps, *Human Nature in the Bible* (New York: Charles Scribner's Sons, 1922).

10. Vidal v. Girard's Executors, 43 U.S. 127 (1844).
11. Wayne Grudem, *Politics According to the Bible* (Grand Rapids, MI: Zondervan, 2010), 23–54.
12. Winston Churchill, quoted in Richard M. Langworth, ed., *Churchill by Himself: The Definitive Collection of Quotations* (New York: Public Affairs, 2008), 573.
13. John Newton, *The Works of the Rev. John Newton* (London: Nathan Whiting, 1824), 466.

Chapter 9: A More Perfect Union

1. William Penn, quoted in Jerry R. Self, *America's God and Its Founding Fathers* (New York: Vantage Press, Inc., 2009), 146.
2. Quoted in Michael Holler, *The Constitution Made Easy* (New York: Sterling, 2012), 42.
3. James Madison, quoted in Earl Taylor, ed., *The Founders' Unchanging Principles of Liberty*, National Center for Constitutional Studies, https://www.nccs.net/2004-07-the-founders-unchanging-principles-of-liberty.php.
4. Ronald Reagan, "Ronald Reagan's Farewell Speech," PBS, http://www.pbs.org/wgbh/americanexperience/features/primary-resources/reagan-farewell/.
5. Laura Hudson, "Superman Renounces U.S. Citizenship in 'Action Comics' #900," *Comics Alliance*, http://comicsalliance.com/superman-renounces-us-citizenship.
6. Ibid.

Chapter 10: The Courts and Christianity

1. Ronald Reagan, Proclamation 5018 (February 3, 1983).
2. See resources at http://vftonline.org/EndTheWall/TrinityHistory.htm.
3. Abraham Lincoln, speech at Kalamazoo, Michigan, August 27, 1856, in Roy P. Blaser, ed., *The Collected Works of Abraham Lincoln* (Brunswick, NJ: Rutgers University Press, 1953–55), 2:366.
4. *Time Magazine* (February 14, 1954).
5. Noah Webster, *History of the United States* (New-Haven: Durrie & Peck, 1832), 6.
6. Noah Webster, *Letters to a Young Gentleman Commencing His Education* (New Haven: Howe & Spalding, 1823).
7. John Quincy Adams, *Letters of John Quincy Adams to His Son on the Bible and Its Teachings* (Auburn, NY: Derby, Miller & Co., 1848), 61, 70–71.
8. Quoted in Lucy N. Oliveri, ed., *Ten Commandments: Supreme Court Opinion and Briefs with Indexes* (New York: Nova Science Publishers, Inc., 2006), 72.

9. Brian Duignan, "The Ten Worst U.S. Supreme Court Decisions, Part One," *Encyclopedia Britannica online*, http://www.britannica.com/list/editor-picks-the-10-worst-u.s.-supreme-court-decisions-%28part-one%29.

10. Hammer v. Dagenhart, 247 U.S. 251 (1918).

11. "Korematsu v. United States, 1944," http://college.cengage.com/history/ayers_primary_sources/korematsu_unitedstates1944.htm. Source: *United States Reports: Cases Adjudged in the Supreme Court at October Term, 1944, October 2, 1944, to and including January 29, 1945*, vol. 323 (Washington: Government Printing Office, 1945), 214-224.

12. Ronald Regan, "Proclamations, February 3, 1983," *The Public Papers of President Ronald W. Reagan*, Ronald Reagan Presidential Library, https://reaganlibrary.archives.gov/archives/speeches/1983/20383b.htm.

13. George Müller, *A Narrative of Some of the Lord's Dealing with George Müller, Written by Himself, Jehovah Magnified. Addresses by George Müller Complete and Unabridged*, 2 vols. (Muskegon, MI: Dust and Ashes, 2003), 1:272–73.

14. John Winthrop, quoted in Kimberly Winston, "From Theological Tenet to Political Password," *Beliefnet*, www.beliefnet.com/story/139/story_13917_1.html.

Chapter 11: Wake Up, Church

1. "A Statement from Jim Bob and Michelle Duggar, and Josh Duggar," The Duggar Family (Michelle's blog), August 20, 2015, http://www.duggarfamily.com/2015/8/statements-from-jim-bob-and-michelle-duggar-and-josh-duggar.

2. C. S. Lewis, *The Screwtape Letters* (New York: Macmillan, 1943), 61.

3. "Christian pollster sheds new light on what church-goers want preached from the pulpit," on Glenn Beck's website, updated September 23, 2015, http://www.glennbeck.com/2015/09/23/christian-pollster-sheds-new-light-on-what-church-goers-want-preached-from-the-pulpit/?utm_source=glennbeck&utm_medium=contentcopy_link.

Chapter 12: Your Role in Restoring America's True Greatness

1. Ronald W. Reagan, quoted in Phil Gailey, "Reagan, at Prayer Breakfast, Calls Politics and Religion Inseparable," *New York Times*, August 24, 1984, http://www.nytimes.com/1984/08/24/us/reagan-at-prayer-breakfast-calls-politics-and-religion-inseparable.html.

2. Woodrow Wilson (1828–1954, twenty-eighth president of the US), in a speech delivered in Denver, Colorado, on May 7, 1911.

3. Ulysses S. Grant, quoted by Henry H. Halley, *Halley's Bible Handbook* (Grand Rapids, MI: Regency Reference Library, 1962), 18.

4. Ronald W. Reagan, quoted in Phil Gailey, "Reagan, at Prayer Breakfast, Calls Politics and Religion Inseparable," *The New York Times*, August 24, 1984, http://www.nytimes.com/1984/08/24/us/reagan-at-prayer-break-fast-calls-politics-and-religion-inseparable.html.

5. Abraham Lincoln, "Proclamation 97: Appointing a Day of National Humiliation, Fasting, and Prayer," March 30, 1863, The American Presidency Project, http://www.presidency.ucsb.edu/was/?pid=69891.

6. Erwin Lutzer, *Is God on America's Side? The Surprising Answer and How It Affects Our Future* (Chicago: Moody Publishers, 2008), 76.

7. Abraham Lincoln, "First Inaugural Address of Abraham Lincoln," March 4, 1861, Lillian Goldman Law Library, http://avalon.law.yale.edu/19th_century/lincoln1.asp.

8. Joel C. Rosenberg, *Implosion: Can America Recover from Its Economic and Spiritual Challenges in Time?* (Carol Stream, IL: Tyndale Publishing, 2012), 338.

9. Jacob Duché, "First Prayer of the Continental Congress, 1774," US House of Representatives, Office of the Chaplain, http://chaplain.house.gov/archive/continental.html.

Chapter 13: Take a Stand

1. A statement accredited to Christian thinker Charles Colson (1931–2012).

2. Christian Smith and Melissa Lundquist Denton, quoted in Gene Edward Veith, "A Nation of Deists," *WORLD Magazine*, June 25, 2005, http://www.worldmag.com/2005/06/a_nation_of_deists.

Appendix 1: A Road Map to Restoring America

1. C. H. Spurgeon, quoted in Ron Rhodes, *1001 Unforgettable Quotes About God, Faith, and the Bible* (Eugene, OR: Harvest House Publishers, 2011), 854.

ABOUT THE AUTHORS

Jason Jimenez

Jason Jimenez is a pastor, apologist, author, and national speaker who has ministered to families for nearly twenty years. In his extensive ministry career, Jason has been a Children's, Student, College, and Family Pastor. He has spent a great deal of time investing in marriages, improving families, discipling young people, and equipping parents to be more effective in their homes.

Jason has founded many non-profit organizations designed to work alongside churches and families, and help them grow strong in the knowledge and advancement of Christianity.

Jason is the Founder and President of Stand Strong Ministries, a national organization that reinforces Christians with a biblical worldview. He also cohosts *Viral Truth* with Alex McFarland, a TV show which reaches millions of homes each week on NRB TV, as well as traveling all over America with their STAND STRONG tours (a biblical worldview movement that emboldens churches to know and defend the Christian faith). Jason's ministry has received praise from some of the world's greatest Christian leaders (such as Ravi Zacharias, Norman Geisler, and Josh McDowell). He has studied at the University of Arizona in philosophy, is a graduate of Southern Evangelical Seminary, and has extensively studied theology and apologetics at Veritas Evangelical Seminary.

Jason is the author of *The Raging War of Ideas: How to Take Back Our Faith, Family, and Country*, and coauthored with Dr.

Norman Geisler *The Official Study Guide to I Don't Have Enough Faith to Be an Atheist* and *The Bible's Answers to 100 of Life's Biggest Questions,* published by Baker Books. He has been married to Celia since 2001, and together, they have four beautiful children.

Alex McFarland

As a speaker, writer, and advocate for apologetics, Alex McFarland has spoken in hundreds of locations throughout the US and abroad. He has preached in over fifteen hundred different churches throughout North America and internationally, and has been featured at conferences, such as The Billy Graham School of Evangelism, Focus On The Family's *Big Dig*, Josh McDowell's *True Foundations* events, California's *Spirit West Coast*, and many more.

He has been interviewed on *Fox and Friends* (the most widely watched morning show in the US), the *Alan Colmes Show*, Fox News' "*The Strategy Room*," Billy Graham's *Decision* radio broadcast, by James Dobson (Focus On The Family radio), NPR's *All Things Considered*, *New York Times*, *Washington Post*, Chuck Colson's *Breakpoint* broadcast, CBS, FOX, NBC News, SRN News, the Associated Press (AP) wire service, *LA Times*, *Boston Herald*, the BBC, *OK-Celebrity News Magazine*, *Prime Time America*, CBN, CSPAN, Bible Broadcast Network, *La Vie* (France), *Christianity Today*, *Charisma*, *On Mission*, and numerous other media outlets as well. In a 2009 story, CNN called Alex McFarland "an expert on world religions and cults."

During the 1990s (at a time when it was predicted that the need for apologetics was waning), Alex pioneered apologetics conference formats designed to equip teens and adults to defend their faith. Attendees of all ages began to attend Alex's "Truth For A New Generation" and "National Conference On Christian Apologetics" events, eagerly learning from a variety of scholars, such as Josh McDowell, Ravi Zacharias and Lee Strobel.

In 2006 Alex was named third president of Southern Evangelical Seminary. During his tenure of nearly five years, Alex led the school through a number of important initiatives. These included fundraising and construction of a new classroom building, development of a national marketing strategy (which contributed to a doubling of student enrollment), the creation of several new degree programs, expansion of staff, and the launching of an online bookstore for the school. Prior to this, Alex had served as Focus On The Family's Director of Teen Apologetics.

In his home state of North Carolina, the Jaycees named Alex one of "Forty Leaders Under The Age of Forty." Alex is the only evangelist known to have preached in all fifty states in only fifty days, through his "Tour Of Truth." This speaking tour across America included sixty-four evangelistic services, became the subject of Alex's first book, and was used by God to bring many people to personal faith in Christ.

During the past decade, Alex has hosted two nationally syndicated radio broadcasts, *Truth Talk Live* (2000–2010) and *SoundRezn* radio (2009–2010). In 2011, Alex became cohost of *Explore the Word,* which is heard weekdays in the nearly two hundred markets served by the American Family Radio Network. He also cohosts the weekly television program "Viral Truth" with Jason Jimenez on the National Religious Broadcasters network.

As a broadcaster, Alex provides on-air teaching, fields live questions from listeners, and has interviewed hundreds of notable guests. These have included a variety of Christian leaders (such as James Dobson, Chuck Colson, George Barna, Tony Campolo, Ravi Zacharias, and Franklin Graham), political newsmakers (such as Mike Huckabee, Michelle Bauchman, Rick Santorum, Maggie Gallagher, and Judge Roy Moore), skeptics (Christopher Hitchens, Michael Shermer), and musicians (such as Brian Wilson of the Beach Boys, and Grammy winners Marilyn McCoo and Billy Davis, Jr.).

As an author, Alex McFarland has written over one hundred and fifty published articles and is the author of sixteen books, including *The Ten Most Common Objections to Christianity* (Regal), and *STAND STRONG in College* (Focus On The Family / Tyndale). In 2009, Tyndale publishers released three new titles by Alex in his *STAND* series. These are: *STAND: Diving Into God's Word (a look at Psalm 119); STAND: Unleashing the Wisdom of God (a look at the book of Proverbs);* and *STAND: Seeking the Ways of God (a look at the life of Joseph).*

In the summer of 2010, Alex McFarland and Elmer Towns (Dean of Liberty University) released their book *10 Questions Every Christian Must Answer* (Broadman & Holman Academic, Spring 2011). During the months of May and July 2010, this was a "featured resource" in all Lifeway Christian Stores.

Alex McFarland attended the University of North Carolina at Greensboro, and earned a Master's degree in Christian Thought/ Apologetics from Liberty University. He was awarded an honorary Doctor of Divinity degree by Southern Evangelical Seminary in 2006. In 2009, Alex studied further in the select program *Developing Young Leaders In Higher Education¾* a "by invitation only" study program at Harvard University.

Alex is the co-director of Stand Strong Ministries, a national organization that reinforces Christians with a biblical worldview. He also cohosts *Viral Truth* with Jason Jimenez, a TV show which reaches millions of homes each week on NRB TV, as well as traveling all over America with their STAND STRONG tours.

Angie McFarland is the godly and supportive wife who has played a tremendous role in all that the Lord has called Alex to do. They have been married since 1988 and currently live in North Carolina.

StandStrongMinistries.org